MEXICO AND THE UNITED STATES

The Fragile Relationship

Twayne's International History Series

Akira Iriye, editor
Harvard University

MEXICO AND THE UNITED STATES

The Fragile Relationship

Lester D. Langley
The University of Georgia

TWAYNE PUBLISHERS • BOSTON
A DIVISION OF G.K. HALL & CO.

Copyright 1991 by Lester D. Langley
All rights reserved
Published by Twayne Publishers
A division of G. K. Hall & Co.
70 Lincoln Street, Boston, Massachusetts 02111

Twayne's International History Series, No. 8

Designed by Barbara Anderson
Produced by Gabrielle B. McDonald
Copyediting supervised by Barbara Sutton

The paper used in this publication meets the minimum requirements
of American National Standard for Information Sciences—Permanence
of Paper for Printed Library Materials, ANSI Z39.48-1984. ∞™

Printed and bound in the United States of America.

Library of Congress Cataloging-in-Publication Data

Langley, Lester D.
    Mexico and the United States : the fragile relationship / Lester
  D. Langley.
        p.   cm.—(Twayne's international history series ; no. 8)
    Includes bibliographical references and index.
    ISBN 0-8057-7912-4 (hc).—ISBN 0-8057-9209-0 (pb)
    1. United States—Foreign relations—Mexico. 2. Mexico—Foreign
  relations—United States. 3. United States—Foreign
  relations—1945– 4. Mexico—Foreign relations—1946–   I. Title.
  II. Series.
  E183.8.M6L283   1991
  327.73072—dc20   90-28114
                                                                     CIP

10 9 8 7 6 5 4 3 2 1 (hc)
10 9 8 7 6 5 4 3 2 1 (pb)

For

Lucía Rede Madrid

*Who lives in Redlands, Texas, a few
hundred yards from the Rio Grande, and
has known the harshness of life on the
border that divides two nations, two cultures,
and two peoples,
But who is not embittered and believes
in One America.*

and

Dr. Charles Knapp

*Who served in the Department of Labor in
the administration of President Jimmy Carter
and tried to reconcile the needs of U.S.
business with the compassion of the
American people for those who come here
to labor and to achieve the American dream*

CONTENTS

Epilogue

ILLUSTRATIONS

Photographs follow page 73

FOREWORD

Twayne's International History Series seeks to publish reliable and readable accounts of post-World War II international affairs. Today, nearly 50 years after the end of the war, the time seems opportune for a critical assessment of world affairs on the second half of the twentieth century. What themes and trends have characterized international relations since 1945? How have they evolved and changed? What connections have developed between international and domestic affairs? How have states and peoples defined and pursued their objectives, and what have they contributed to the world at large? How have conceptions of warfare and visions of peace changed?

These questions must be addressed if one is to arrive at an understanding of the contemporary world that is international—with an awareness of the linkages among different parts of the world—as well as historical—with a keen sense of what the immediate past has brought to civilization. Hence Twayne's *International History* Series. It is hoped that the volumes in this series will help the reader to explore important events and decisions since 1945 and to develop the global awareness and historical sensitivity required for confronting today's problems.

The first volumes in the series examine the United States' relations with other countries, groups of countries, or regions. The focus on the United States is justified in part because of the nation's predominant position in postwar international relations, and also because far more extensive documentation is available on American foreign affairs than is the case with other countries. The series addresses not only those interested in international relations, but also those studying America's and other countries' histories, who will find here useful guides and fresh insights into the recent past. Now more than ever, it is imperative to understand the linkages between national history and international history.

This volume offers a truly binational perspective in describing U.S.—Mexican relations since World War II. Lester Langley, a leading historian of these relations, shows how important it is to observe this bilateral relationship in the context of the intermeshing of the two societies, two peoples. If the United States has had a major impact on Mexican politics and society, so has Mexico transformed American society through immigration, trade, and other interactions. In a sense, then, U.S.–Mexican relations are exemplary of the gradual globalization of national affairs that has so characterized postwar history. The reader is well advised to follow Professor Langley's richly detailed descriptions with a view to understanding the forces that are shaping the contemporary world.

Akira Iriye

PREFACE

When Akira Iriye inquired about my interest in writing a book on U.S.–Mexican relations for Twayne's International History Series, I was both flattered and a bit perplexed. In earlier works I had explored U.S. relations with the Caribbean Basin from the American Revolution until the present and had written a book on American military interventions in the first third of the twentieth century. But save for limited research on the French intervention in Mexico in the 1860s and the U.S. military's occupation of Veracruz in 1914, I had done little on Mexico. What prompted me to accept the opportunity to write a book on U.S.–Mexican affairs was Dr. Iriye's highly acclaimed reputation among diplomatic historians for looking beyond the strategic calculations that preoccupy our profession to political, economic, and especially cultural factors that deeply influence policy. At the time of his invitation I was completing two works that in different ways reflect this approach: *America and the Americas: The United States in the Western Hemisphere* (1989) and *MexAmerica: Two Countries, One Future* (1988), which complements this study.

Relations between the United States and Mexico are of vital importance, particularly in the years since 1945, and will remain so. By 2000, it is estimated, the *real* border between these two countries—which extends for 100 miles on either side of the legal demarcation—will be the most populated area in North America. Indeed, Mexico and the Caribbean Basin constitute the most vital region in U.S. defense strategy. The United States not only shares a 2,000-mile border with Mexico (over which 500,000 legal crossings are made every day) but the two countries' economies are virtually intertwined. The average American (Mexicans politely demur at our appropriation of "American" to mean a resident of the United States, preferring "North American") looks at Mexico as a country of debt, poverty, and corruption. Undeniably, Mexico staggers under a heavy foreign debt (and a more burdensome internal debt), seemingly unbridgeable gaps between rich and poor (the "two Mexicos" remains a common descriptive phrase), and undeniable official corruption.

But there is "another Mexico." Thirteenth in land area and eleventh in population

among the world's nations, Mexico is a formidable economic presence, or so concluded a 1988 staff assessment prepared for the Joint Economic Committee of the U.S.
Congress. It ranks fourth among proven oil reserves, has a diversified agricultural
sector, and produces more manufactured goods than Taiwan or South Korea. It is fifth
among suppliers of U.S. imports (the United States imports 11 percent of its oil from
Mexico) and third (after Canada and Japan) as a destination for U.S. exports. U.S.
investments occupy 80 percent of the total foreign investment portfolio in Mexico.[1]
President Carlos Salinas de Gortari, elected in 1988, has reversed Mexico's official
suspicion of the foreign, especially U.S., economic intrusion and is championing free
trade with the United States and more foreign investment. If achieved, the North
American trade area will have 350 million people, more numerous and potentially
stronger than the European Community. Mexico in 2000, reported Polyconomics (a
New Jersey economic research firm) has the resources and capability to become "another Taiwan."[2]

Our ties with Mexico go beyond the economic realm. One third of the United
States was carved from one half of Mexico. Over the years, as two economies became
more visibly linked, the migration of Mexicans north has strengthened the Mexican
ethnic and cultural presence in the United States. Today, some 75% of Hispanics,
U.S.A.—15 of 20 million Americans—are of Mexican heritage. More significantly,
in recent years Mexicans and Mexican Americans (or Chicanos), once mutually
disdainful, have become more conscious of their "familial" ties. The United States has
shaped Mexico's history, most Americans know; but too few realize Mexico's claim on
our history.

Despite these economic and cultural links, many Americans are unmindful of the
"Mexican connection" or, if assessing Mexican-United States relations, are often
critical or troubled about what is happening in Mexico. Their befuddlement is understandable, given the contradictory patterns in Mexico's economic and political history
since 1940. For the past fifty years, for example, Mexican elections have offered a
sometimes striking contrast to the Latin American norm in their regularity and legitimacy, yet domination of the electoral process by the official party (Partido Revolucionario Institucional, or PRI) and widespread electoral fraud have persuaded some
Americans that Mexico is no closer to democracy now than in 1940. Mexico's economic growth since 1940 has been remarkable, making possible the Mexican "economic miracle" of the forties and fifties and the growth of an impressive middle-class,
yet modern Mexico has disturbing social inequities. The gap between rich and poor in
Mexico has not narrowed significantly since 1940, despite Mexico's rise to a middle-
level economic power, increases in life expectancy, and impressive achievements in
education.

In the 1980s, of course, the cumulative burdens of debt, social inequities, and
political discontent among Mexico's middle class (which suffered a 50% decline in
living standards during the decade) and leftist political elements precipitated what
Mexicans have named *la crisis*. In the presidential election of 1988, the bitterness and
division among Mexicans about the cause of the nation's economic and social condition attracted considerable press attention in the United States and persuaded some
Americans that Mexicans could never solve their social and economic problems until
Mexico modernized its politics.

There are reassuring signs that Mexico is becoming more democratic, but resolution of its social inequities will require both Mexicans and Americans to address the social problems that have developed with the linking of two economies. These are most visible on the 2,000-mile U.S.-Mexican border, where the "boom times" have reappeared in the early 1990s, creating jobs but also chaotic social conditions in a region of 10 million or, if the respective border-state population is the measure, more than sixty million. Americans believe that the co-existence of economic growth and social inequities is peculiar to third-world nations and reassure themselves that, although the mushrooming squatter colonies may be visible from the American side of the border, such lamentable social problems do not afflict the United States. A close examination of the social condition in this country, I argue in this book, proves to be more disturbing. In looking at such things as the problem of a permanent underclass and the widespread apprehension among middle-class Americans that their children may suffer a lower standard of living, we may have much in common with Mexicans.

Mexico and the United States integrates the lasting features of the two countries' relationship before World War II with the realities of their modern diplomatic, economic, and cultural experience. Thus I not only deal with governmental issues or border problems but also probe the dynamics of a material culture on collision course with a traditional one, the Hispanic (largely Mexican-American) imprint on America, and the reach of the U.S. economy into Mexico. In sum, my purpose is to get student and citizen to think differently about Mexico, to recognize it as not simply a place to visit or invest in but as a country with a greater claim to a share of our national heritage than any other save for Great Britain.

A history of modern U.S.-Mexican relations cannot be written in the traditional fashion of diplomatic history, that is, as a series of unfolding events, disputes, and crises, and the resolution of conflict between governments. History and geography have bound Mexico and the United States in a relationship that each believes diminishes its sovereignty and sense of national identity. To be sure, Mexicans are more outspoken about the frustrations wrought by their country's "special relationship" with its more powerful neighbor, but, ironically, Americans are often fretful about Mexico's defiance of U.S. guidance, however well intentioned, and fearful that Mexican political instability and economic debility will jeopardize U.S. security in this hemisphere.

Nevertheless, the two have fashioned an interdependent border economy where Mexicans and Americans, respectively, conscious of these economic bonds, blend cooperation with spirited nationalism. Theirs is a union not of common purpose or understanding but of necessity. On a score of issues they must and do cooperate, yet their respective leaders, it is sometimes said, not only speak different languages but attach different meanings and interpretations to the same thing. President Jimmy Carter, who speaks Spanish and demonstrated uncommon American admiration for Mexico, to his dismay learned that despite myriad issues that both governments *must* address, the United States government did not have what could be defined as a Mexican policy. His Mexican counterpart (José López Portillo), by contrast, shared with his predecessors a determination to break what many Mexicans regard as demeaning and crippling bonds with their northern neighbor.

How two nations arrived at this juncture in their disparate historical evolution is the subject of this book.

ACKNOWLEDGMENTS

So many scholars and officials on both sides of the border have assisted me in research-
ing and writing this book that I could not list them all, but at least I should identify a
few: Akira Iriye, who asked me to write this book for Twayne's International History
Series; Meghan Robinson Wander, Carol Chin, and especially Barbara Sutton, my
editors at Twayne; Joe Key, Vice-President for Research, University of Georgia, for
assistance in my successful application for a summer stipend from the National Endowment for the Humanities; Robert Pastor, Emory University and the Carter Center, one
of this country's most astute observers of United States-Mexican relations; and several
Mexican colleagues, especially Angela Moyana Pahissa, Jorge Chabat, and Jesús
Tamayo, three of the growing number of U.S. specialists in Mexico.

   My colleague, Thomas Whigham, and Mark Gilderhus, Colorado State University,
read the manuscript. For their assessment, I am grateful.

chapter 1

TWO REPUBLICS, DIFFERENT FUTURES

The Mexican–U.S. relationship has been an uneasy one from the beginning, explained by the circumstances of Mexican independence (which postdated that of the United States by almost 40 years) and exacerbated by the antagonism of political cultures and, most visibly, by a quarter-century conflict for the domination of North America.

The Spanish crown's acceptance of Mexican independence in 1821 was not a triumph of revolution but a political settlement between elites—royalist and Creole—to end a decade of debilitating guerrilla war. Save for the dissolution of the Spanish bureaucracy, Mexico changed little in its political and not at all in its social character. Its legislature was composed of men of landed aristocracy, wealth, and privilege. With the military intact and the church insistent on a special place in the new order, the political culture wrought by independence appeared fixed and unchangeable. The promise of republican governance and its institutions, which had swept the declining Spanish empire, had drawn its strength from British liberalism and the American struggle for independence. But the victorious Creoles in Mexico and elsewhere in Latin America experienced a more fearful example of revolution's legacy: the social conflict born of demands from those below.

Undermined by rumors of a Spanish reconquest, the first government fell within a year (as had the French revolutionary republic) to the imperial pretender. In Mexico Agustín de Iturbide became putative ruler of an empire stretching from the 42nd parallel deep into Central America. But it was an empire with distant, expansive frontiers in the north and defiant ones to the south. The economy, ruined by the many years of revolutionary struggle, shortly collapsed before the demands of Mexican federalists who looked north for their model of government.

As in the United States, Mexico's first generation of political leaders were elitists of varying persuasion: conservatives who wanted the reassurance of executive rule, an established church, and the preservation of class privilege; liberals who professed states' rights, religious tolerance, and egalitarianism. Politics was combative, factional, and personalistic, as was the case in the United States during this period. In the Mexico of the 1820s and 1830s, however, there was no parallel democratic surge from a demanding yeoman class, no romantic fascination with the "blessings of republican liberty," no expansive confidence in national destiny. The factions did not develop into evolving political parties capable of shaping a republican political culture. Mexicans had created political institutions, but their faith resided in the men who exercised power.

Confronted with a vigorous, expansionist republic that directly threatened Mexico's thinly populated northern frontier, the Mexicans initially adopted a generous immigration policy for Anglo settlers in Texas in the naive belief they would become Catholic and Mexican in thought as well as deed. Ownership of Mexican soil did not create a sense of Mexican identity in the Anglo settlers, nor did the settlers' extensive landholdings serve as an effective buffer against their land-hungry countrymen north of the border. Recognizing the failure of its policy, the Mexican government enacted measures to shield the province from American pressures and to exercise stronger controls over it from Mexico City. Centralization, of course, inflamed the thoroughly un-Mexicanized Anglos who, with the support of Mexican federalists, raised the flag of rebellion in 1835. The Texas rebellion's widespread popularity in the United States convinced the Mexicans that the war was, at bottom, a conspiracy hatched in Washington. President Andrew Jackson had, after all, denounced the Transcontinental Treaty of 1819 (which had set the U.S.–Mexican boundary at the Red River), pressed the Mexicans to sell the province (together with California north of Monterey Bay), and applauded those Americans who rushed to Texas's colors in 1835. The Mexican government was not mollified by Jackson's reluctance to champion Texas's annexation as a state. Astute observers will see that political self-interest not recognition of Mexico's rights inspired Jackson's position. His ambivalence over the annexation of Texas had more to do with his desire to avoid confronting the politically divisive issue of the expansion of slavery than with executive appreciation of another nation's sovereignty.

Mexico emerged from the Texas rebellion an embittered, unreconciled neighbor, what historian David Pletcher has appropriately called the "sick man of North America."[1] Its wartime leader, Gen. Antonio López de Santa Anna, had suffered a humiliating defeat at San Jacinto in 1836 and in order to save his life signed over the province to the rebel and Texan forces. To sue for peace, Santa Anna visited Washington with Texas agents. On his return to

Mexico both he and his concessions to the Texans were publicly denounced. Two years later a foreign intervention gave him the opportunity to regain stature among his compatriots. In retaliation for abuses suffered by French merchants in Mexico City, French forces assaulted Veracruz. Santa Anna, the "Crimson Jester," led the city's defenses. In the battle he lost his leg but regained public adulation. Mexican leaders publicly boasted of a *reconquista* and denounced Texas independence. The Mexican government refused to recognize the Republic of Texas and disputed its claim to territory bordered by the Rio Grande. In 1842 a Mexican army defended Santa Fe against an expedition of warring Texans.

Already, however, the United States had become alert to twin menaces involving both Texas and Mexico. The first was an exaggerated but perceived threat from British abolitionism, which had triumphed in the West Indies and pressed upon an independent Texas with increasing economic ties to British textiles. The second, more complex menace was the implication of the French–British–Mexican barrier to the United States' newly addressed commitment to "manifest destiny"—to spread the "blessings of republican liberty" across the North American continent. France supplied military advisors to the Texans, and the French foreign minister, François Guizot, aroused his countrymen with talk of a North American balance of power and French colonists on the Texas prairie. The Texans rejected a French proposal to construct a series of forts, which disheartened Guizot, but the British, under the prodding of Lord Aberdeen, almost immediately began cultivating the Texans with promises of loans and pressing the Mexicans to recognize Texas independence. Coupled with the menace of Texas "Africanization" (a free-labor economic system), the European challenge was sufficient to revive demands for Texas's immediate annexation. In the 1844 presidential election, the Democratic candidate, James Knox Polk, responding to western pressures, vowed to resolve the dual North American territorial disputes with Great Britain over Oregon and deal forcefully with Mexico over California and Texas. Although Polk's rhetoric about Oregon was more bellicose, he was predisposed to compromise with Great Britain and prepared to enter a war with Mexico.[2]

In identifying Mexico as a greater menace than Great Britain to the nation's manifest destiny, Polk cleverly distracted the American public from Oregon, where he was prepared to yield, to California and Texas, where he wasn't. A parallel compromise there was out of the question. France and especially Britain were acquiescing in the nation's self-professed mission in North America; Mexico, in predictably obstinate fashion, was not. Its diplomatic intransigence, thus, warranted a forceful response. In 1845 President Polk dispatched a special minister, John Slidell, to Mexico City to purchase California and New Mexico and to persuade the Mexican government to accept the reality of Texas statehood. Secretary of State James Buchanan instructed Slidell that the United States would not "tolerate any interference on the part of European sovereigns with controversies in America, [nor] permit them to apply the worn-out dogma of the balance of power to the free States of the Continent. . . . Liberty here must be allowed to work out its natural results; and these will, ere long, astonish the world."[3]

Buchanan thus invoked the use of force in the cause of republican liberty. Chastising the British and French governments for their error in trying to reconcile Mexico and the Texas republic—a not altogether fanciful diplomatic effort—the president dispatched secret agents to Texas to coax the wavering Texans into finally voting for statehood. When the more belligerent Mexican government of Gen. Juan Paredes summarily rejected Polk's final offer to purchase California and New Mexico, the president prepared a war message, citing the longstanding disputes over the U.S.–Mexican boundary, unresolved claims, and Mexican diplomatic intransigence.

Polk wanted California and feared that the grumbling Californios would emulate the Texans and secede from the Mexican republic before the United States could lay claim to the province. He had alertly dispatched the army under Gen. John Fremont to the northern California border and was apparently ready to make war to prevent the creation of a Bear Flag Republic. And in January 1846 Polk had sent Gen. Zachary Taylor and his regiment across the Nueces and on to the Rio Grande, into territory claimed by the Texans but not yet incorporated into the republic. For a few months there was an odd stand-off between Mexican and American armies encamped on opposite sides of the Rio Grande. In May, Mexican forces unable to tolerate the intrusion any longer, crossed the river and, as President Polk dramatically reported to Congress, "shed American blood upon the American soil." News of the skirmish between a superior Mexican force and some of Taylor's dragoons enabled Polk to alter the war message he was already preparing: he could thus blame Mexico for beginning a war that he, in fact, had provoked.

Not a few Americans, especially in New England, believed that Polk precipitated war with Mexico in order to expand slavery's domain. But as long as the president conducted what many saw as a "defensive" war to safeguard Texas and incorporate largely unsettled southwestern territories, the political malcontents could do little to stop it. Until February 1847, Polk skillfully confined war operations to northern Mexico, New Mexico, and California, which U.S. military forces invaded by land and by sea. Still, the Mexicans did not capitulate, and the president fell back to essentially the same strategy as Mexico's Spanish conquerors in 1519, a landing at Veracruz and a plunge into the populous central highlands. Outwitted by Santa Anna (who had duped the president into believing that, if subsidized, he would return to Mexico and negotiate a satisfactory settlement), faced with revived Mexican fighting spirit, and furious over the "penny-press" attention given to his generals, especially Taylor, Polk dispatched Gen. Winfield Scott to seize the Mexican capital and wrest a settlement. By September, Scott's invaders had finally conquered the Aztec citadel, and for all purposes, the war was over.

Official peace did not come until the following February, when a discredited State Department official, Nicholas Trist, exceeded his instructions and signed a treaty with a Mexican peace delegation that had, frankly, no clear authority to deal with him. By now, Polk the commander in chief was entertaining fleeting notions of annexing all Mexico. A quick congressional acceptance of Trist's treaty, which in fact satisfied U.S. objectives in 1846, grounded Polk's ambitions, however. In the Senate, a gaggle of Southern Democrats apprehensive about a "Presidential War" and Whigs who thought both Polk and the war distasteful joined forces to approve the peace settlement. In the aftermath the secessionist Yucatán, where a murderous caste war had broken out earlier in the decade, made an unusual appeal to the United States, Spain, and Great Britain for "protection" from Mexico. There was a momentary resuscitation of annexationist fever, especially in the South, on the mistaken belief that the Yucatán was ideally suited for cotton production. As this zeal dissipated, Polk used the Monroe doctrine, which he had already applied to California, a second time to warn the Yucatecos that they could not voluntarily make the province a European protectorate.

Thus ended (if one does not count the incursion into Canada during the war of 1812) the United States' first foreign war. Mexico lost half its national domain; the United States lost for at least a century its image as a "model republic" of the Western Hemisphere. For most Americans, the war reaffirmed the romantic notions of the age about manifest destiny and mission—however much these were tainted with blatantly racist beliefs—and guaranteed a republican future for North America. A small coterie of Mexican Liberals, who believed the loss would expunge militarism and its attendant evils from the republic, quietly welcomed the humiliation. Several emerging Republican leaders, notably Abraham Lincoln, a young congressman when the war began, and Ulysses S. Grant, who served in the invasion of Mexico, feared the sudden accumulation of Mexican domain would transform the United States into an empire and degrade its republican institutions. But most Americans tolerated or shared the opinion promoted by the *New York Herald* at the moment of triumph: the American victory had guaranteed the nation a lofty place in the "history of civilization and the human race."[4]

Latin American governments, mindful of U.S. territorial aggrandizement, revealed some apprehension over continental expansionism at the 1856 Pan American conference in Santiago. Mexico, however, was not dramatically elevated in hemispheric estimation as the altogether undeserving victim of American aggression, nor did the United States become a pariah nation to South America's political savants. Juan Alberdi, the Argentine statesman, praised England and the United States as the guardians of freedom. His fellow Argentine, Domingo Sarmiento, who visited the United States and wrote a biography of Abraham Lincoln, chastised his countrymen who condemned the predatory Yankees: "Let us not detain the United States in its march."[5]

With their humiliation Mexicans reached into their past and returned to power Santa Anna. The Crimson Jester promptly sold more of the nation's domain—the Mesilla Valley, in southern Arizona, for $10 million—and took on the attributes and habits of a monarch. In 1855 he was driven from power, and Mexico fell into a bitter civil war between Liberals, who railed against the military and the church and their privileges, and Conservatives, who yearned to return a "heathen republic" to a properly monarchical state. This and the ensuing struggle in the United States would provide opportunity for two men—Benito Juárez and Abraham Lincoln—who had curiously parallel careers. Juárez, a determined Zapotec Indian from Oaxaca, fought and triumphed over the monarchists and assumed the presidency dressed in somber black just two months before Lincoln himself took the oath. In 1864, when the French installed Maximilian on his Mexican throne, Juárez assumed leadership of a three-year guerrilla war against him and his Mexican supporters.

When the French invaded Mexico, Lincoln was president, and the United States plunged into a civil war, yet the Union maintained fragile but vital links to the Juarista cause. Secretary of State William H. Seward, though not invoking the Monroe Doctrine by name, did remind the French of the republican destiny of the hemisphere. And when Confederate emissaries sought out the continually moving Juárez, they discovered Lincoln's agents had preceded them, not with goods or munitions but with pledges and reminders that the causes of Lincoln and Juárez were parallel struggles. In the last year of the U.S. Civil War, as the Juaristas pressed against the enemy, Juárez's minister to the United States, Matias Romero, roused a Republican Congress on behalf of the Mexican cause. Within months of Lee's surrender, Seward was hounding the French to withdraw from their Mexican enterprise, and triumphant Union officers publicly boasted of readiness to invade northern Mexico. Two years later, Juárez cornered and defeated his enemy in Querétaro and, despite foreign pleas for clemency, ordered the execution of the last pretender to a Mexican throne. Seward had condemned the restoration of monarchism; Juárez and his illiterate mestizos expunged it.[6]

To the north, the United States, its unity guaranteed by the Union triumph, entered the modern industrial era. But for Mexico, civil war and the struggle against monarchism had settled only the issue of foreign intervention, military privilege, and church landholding. Yet to be confronted were still unresolved internal political, economic, and especially social problems. Juárez had triumphed over the European pretender; he could not easily pacify the armies of discontented Juaristas who, like their forebears in the 1820s, looked to reap the profits of their victory. Border problems persisted. As he had always feared, the Americans—using as evidence Mexico's inability to police the northern frontier—demanded that U.S. troops be permitted to cross the border in pursuit of rustlers and Indians. These search parties displayed such zeal that Juárez sensed the Yankees were again preparing to annex Mexican territory. Alertly, the Mexican government noted that rustling worked both ways. Ambitious Anglo cattlemen in south Texas were not only expanding their landholdings by legal trickery and fraudulent surveys—and to the detriment of Mexican Americans—but were also increasing their herds by rustling from their neighbors. It was not until 1876, when disgruntled Juarista officer Porfirio Díaz raised the flag of rebellion against Juárez's successor from the safety of Texas, that relations with the United States became more amicable.

Relations moved in that direction because Díaz, more than any Mexican leader, accurately perceived U.S. priorities in Mexico—political order and economic development. Denied immediate recognition, Díaz pushed for *joint* policing of the border, arguing that if U.S. troops entered Mexico in pursuit of Indians or rustlers, then Mexican troops could cross into U.S. territory for the same purpose. In the beginning, American leaders, mindful of the revival of expansionist sentiment in the country, resisted these entreaties, but it soon became clear that *private* American investors, eager to build rail lines, buy land, or develop mining operations in the north of Mexico, wanted a prompt resolution of U.S.–Mexican problems. Through the remainder of the 1870s, the border situation remained uncertain, but Díaz began cultivating European countries with interests parallel to those of American investors. By 1880, when he handpicked his successor, Manuel González, it was clear that the American government was rethinking its traditional view of Mexico and its leaders.

Díaz's pacification of the always-turbulent Mexican countryside—a policy he pursued with brutal effectiveness—did much to alter Mexico's image among Americans and Europeans alike. His harshness to his own people coupled with the obvious advantage he granted to highly visible foreign investors ultimately inspired the scornful lament, "Mexico is the parent of foreigners and the stepparent of Mexicans." There were still diplomatic irritations over the always-troublesome northern border. When the American government briefly took up the cause of Guatemala in its territorial dispute with Mexico about Chiapas, the southern border became an issue as well. When Díaz returned to the presidency in 1884, more consequential economic links had irretrievably altered U.S.–Mexican relations. The most dramatic was the building of railroads between Mexico City and Ciudad Juárez and Laredo. Together with the surge of American investment in mining and purchases of large tracts of land, the laying of the railroad signalled the incorporation of the Mexican into the more dynamic U.S. economy.

The United States, admired by Mexican Liberals for its republican government, now became Mexico's economic tutor as well. Europe shared with the states the role of social tutor. Hospitable to foreign investment, immigrants, and the Social Darwinist views then widespread in England and the United States, Díaz's Mexico projected the image of a modern, industrial society. By the 1890s, when the government went on the gold standard and its finance ministers conversed readily and easily with European and U.S. bankers,

American observers, accustomed to denigrating Mexico and Mexicans, now provided reassuring stories about American venture capitalists and land barons who had tamed the wilds of the Mexican north. Díaz's prohibition of bullfighting, which foreigners had always cited as evidence of the country's uncivilized social behavior, appeared to validate the encomia.

Yet despite these conspicuous changes, much about Mexico remained unchanged. For one thing, the foreigners (especially Americans) who came to Mexico during these years did not assimilate but rather comported themselves in such an overbearing way as to revive xenophobia and especially anti-Americanism, which had diminished during the 1860s. Even the lowliest perceived that Mexico's sudden arrival as an industrial country had created wealth but only for the privileged. Although Mexico had an impressive network of rail lines by the end of the century, the system linked only cities and thus served consumers and distributors, not the vast numbers who still lived on the land. True, industrialism did create a middle class of merchants and tradesmen in the cities, but it made no market in the countryside and provided scant opportunity for the Mexican peasant—who accounted for about 60 percent of the population—to move up the economic or social ladder. Industry expanded, creating jobs for unskilled and a few skilled workers; latifundia (large landholdings) expanded more vigorously and thus created a rapacious appetite for land and the labor to work on it. Ironically, the Liberal laws of the 1850s that had divested the church of its lands deprived Indians of their only reliable protector and opened up the Mexican countryside—even the *ejidos*, traditional communal holdings—to exploitation by the ambitious. By 1910, when the revolution erupted, 1 percent of the nation's landholders held 97 percent of Mexico's arable land. The grandson of the peon of 1876 was still a peon.[7]

Emulating the industrial model of the United States, Díaz strived to modernize Mexico, but the result was an economy that in 1900 was rapidly falling under the sway of foreigners, especially Americans, who had more than $500 million invested in Mexican railroads, mines, real estate, public debt, oil, banking, and insurance. In the three decades since its own civil conflict, the United States had succeeded in developing an economy and—though not without political discord—bringing its people into the political culture. Mexico had done the first but not the second. Yet given the seeming serenity of the Mexico visible to the outside world in 1900, few observers would have predicted that within the decade the country would be riven by unrest—in the increasingly volatile industrial and mining sectors, where Sindicalists agitated over working conditions; in the South, where the vigorous expansion of the agro-export sector had enslaved a generation of Indian laborers and alienated small farmers; and among middle-class hacendados (landowners) who read Western political thought and dreamed of bringing political, though not social, reforms to twentieth-century Mexico.

Actually, Díaz had encouraged the opposition in the 1890s when he had permitted malcontents to organize into the Liberal Union to identify candidates who might inherit the presidential sash. This was a movement Díaz easily manipulated until 1904, when he cavalierly arranged his own succession. Thereafter, the dissatisfied hesitantly voiced the first muted protests about the presidential succession. The old dictator's interview with the American journalist James Creelman in 1908, in which Díaz casually said that Mexico was ready for democracy, merely served to make his political critics more outspoken. They found their champion in a diminutive Liberal hacendado, Francisco Madero, who abstained from drink and meat and wrote eloquently about a more democratic Mexico in a popular tract, *The Presidential Succession in 1910.*

On his behalf, Mexican reformers commenced a political struggle in 1910 that eventually drove Díaz from power and installed Madero in the presidential chair. But another less visible but no less consequential movement for *social* change had accompanied this long struggle for "effective suffrage and no reelection." Its origins lay in the vast social inequities between rural and urban Mexico. Its disparate leaders spoke incessantly about the rural backwardness wrought in a country ruled according to positivist credos and by a clique of financial advisors known as *científicos.* Some of the rebellious Liberals, like the Flores Magón brothers (Jesús, Enrique, and Ricardo), were social ideologues who found kindred spirits in the Industrial Workers of the World and, like the Wobblies, published socialist tracts (such as *Regeneración*) and advocated such radical solutions to Mexico's problems as minimum wages, nationalization of church property, return of Indian communal lands, seizure of untilled lands, and requirements that foreigners who owned property in Mexico become citizens. By 1906 the social agitators had organized into the Liberal party and called for "land and liberty." For them, political reform was inadequate for resolution of the social ills that plagued the countryside. They found their philosopher in Andrés Molina Enríquez (author of *The Great National Problems*), their leaders in the alienated mestizos, their cause in the rural Mexico that Díaz's long rule had despoiled, and their followers among the landless and the abused.

In 1909 Díaz journeyed to the border and met with President William Howard Taft to discuss, among other things, the political restiveness of middle-class Mexicans. Taft returned to Washington with an uneasy premonition about what was happening in Mexico. Revolution, he feared, might install a more democratic government but in the process threaten the sizable U.S. investment in Mexico. By now Díaz had come to a similar conclusion about the growing discontent, and in the following year the Mexican leader decided that Mexico was not yet ready for the democracy he had apparently pledged in the Creelman interview. He was re-elected in a patently fraudulent election. Mexican Liberals, predictably, expressed polite objections or fled north and proclaimed fiery denunciations. Their protest commenced the Mexican revolution. From the beginning, the United States, though technically neutral, was far more than detached observer of the calamity that ultimately engulfed its neighbor. As Díaz had done in 1876, the enemies of the dictator, the *revoltosos*, took refuge in the United States. Díaz directed his consuls (many strategically located in the U.S. Southwest) to monitor their activities. When the dissidents went underground, he hired private detectives to spy on them. With a curious logic, Díaz surmised that the U.S. government and business concerns with interests in Mexico (Standard Oil among them) were secretly funding the *revoltosos*.

The truth of the matter was that American leaders, though aware of the revolutionaries' presence in the southwest, were only vaguely knowledgeable about what these dissidents were plotting to do. But when Madero—who had challenged Díaz's re-election, was briefly jailed, and then released—fled to the United States to proclaim the cause of effective suffrage and no bossism in Mexico, the United States was suddenly confronted with the possibility that the outburst of violence against Díaz would occur near the border. When, as Americans had feared, the revolution burst forth in northern Mexico, even Madero was taken by surprise. Confident that his troops could deal with the isolated pockets of defiance in the hinterland, Díaz sent them north to Ciudad Juárez. There, in May 1911, as curious El Pasoans sat atop squat buildings and observed, a hastily assembled revolutionary band laid siege to the old dictator's federal garrison and compelled its surrender. Two weeks later, Díaz abandoned Mexico for Paris.

The revolution, most Americans concluded, represented the triumph of Mexican liberalism, and when the diminutive Madero assumed the presidency in November 1911, he pledged to enact its credos of political reform. But for those who viewed Mexico's problems in a social context—as did the Indian peasants of Morelos and Puebla in the South who followed Emiliano Zapata's call for agrarian reform with seizures of land—Madero's compromising demeanor offered little prospect for resolution of *their* revolutionary cause. And, more ominously, Madero's reluctance to punish the enemies within his reach and his apparent nepotism inspired what remained of Diaz's following to hatch conspiracy after conspiracy against him. But despite the explosive violence in the South and the defiant revolutionaries of the North, where the Red Brigades of Pascual Orozoco began their attacks in 1912, Madero survived for more than a year.

The revolution Madero and the Liberals had begun against the old dictator now assumed a character none of them could have foreseen. The social order, forcefully maintained in the long years of Díaz's rule, began to crumble, and Madero had neither the will nor the power to reconstruct it. Historians of these critical days in the revolution still debate whether Madero was undermined by the relentless criticism of U.S. Ambassador Henry Lane Wilson, whose dispatches to Washington characterized Madero as "apathetic, inefficient, cynically indifferent, or stupidly optimistic," or was, more likely, the victim of a military plot.[8] The ambassador became increasingly apprehensive about the safety of Americans and U.S. property in Mexico. Madero's polite rejoinder that Washington was doing too little to contain Mexican rebels operating on U.S. territory was not a satisfactory response.

Just as the situation appeared to be improving in the countryside, Madero fell victim to yet another conspiracy—this one hatched in the army, where a band of conspirators, alert to Madero's forgiving habits, plotted with a couple of revolutionary generals, Bernardo Reyes and Felix Díaz (whom Madero had saved from the firing squad), and raised the flag of rebellion against the president. In such convoluted politics, Ambassador Wilson was no mere diplomatic spectator. Persuaded of Madero's unfitness as Mexico's leader, he called for a stronger U.S. naval presence off Mexico's Gulf coast and propagandized against the Mexican president among Mexico City's fretful diplomatic corps, who joined him in calling for Madero's resignation. Madero courageously refused but now confronted yet another opponent, General Victoriano Huerta, a putatively fearless warrior who fancied liquor and opium. Huerta conspired with Reyes and Felix Díaz to topple the government, even meeting with the latter in the U.S. embassy to conclude the plotting. Madero and his vice president, José María Pino Suárez, were arrested and imprisoned in the National Palace on 17 February 1913. Within the week they were taken out and shot. Two weeks later, Woodrow Wilson, who had condemned the interventionlist policies of his predecessors, took the oath of office as president of the United States.

In the 1912 campaign, Wilson had sharply criticized the two preceding Republican administrations. He faulted the "dollar diplomacy" of Taft and, referring to the large U.S. military intervention in Nicaragua, roundly condemned Theodore Roosevelt for defiling the American foreign tradition by embarking on an imperial course in the Caribbean. After a few months in office, Wilson was championing political reforms for the Dominican Republic and Haiti and, in an oft-cited address in Mobile, Alabama, assured a generation of Latin Americans already weary of the United States playing "policeman" to the hemisphere that his Latin American policy would encroach on neither their sovereignty nor their territory. Mindful of the still-large European economic presence in Latin America, Wilson looked toward a new Pan Americanism, where the commerical ties pledged by Secretary of State Elihu Root in Rio de Janeiro in 1906 (at the third of the modern inter-American conferences) would be strengthened to create a hemisphere shielded from the Old World's political and economic reach by the Monroe Doctrine and the vigor of the expanding U.S. economy.

The president assigned the day-to-day negotiations over salient political and economic problems in Haiti and the Dominican Republic to his former political adversary and now secretary of state, William Jennings Bryan. When the inept but well-intentioned efforts of the "Great Commoner" collapsed a few years later, the president reluctantly approved a military intervention. Wilson chose to handle the more critical Mexican situation himself, partly because he believed his training as a social scientist (although of Anglo-American political institutions) and genuine concern for the welfare of the Mexican people compensated for his ignorance of Mexican political realities, and partly because he considered Mexican policy simply too important to be entrusted to others. Bryan had little conception of the relationship between national interest and national purpose, yet Wilson consciously resisted the bureaucratic pressures from the War Department and from Texas for a military solution, especially on the vulnerable U.S.–Mexican border and in the oil fields around Tampico.

There ensued the policy of "watchful waiting." From the White House came hortatory pronouncements about the Mexican people and their legitimate revolution for political liberty and the betrayal of their cause by Huerta's coup and illegal seizure of power, which merited global condemnation. When the world failed to join him in a moral denuciation of Huerta, Wilson declared that not only would the U.S. government refuse to recognize Huerta but that it would pursue openings to Huerta's political enemies. Wilson thus dispatched the first of a dozen special agents into Mexico to meet with the gaggle of revolutionary leaders who had vaulted to command. Eager to obtain U.S. arms, the revolutionaries responded with predictable condemnations of Huerta as "military usurper." Other governments expressed either bewilderment or amusement at the president's tactics, but Wilson was convinced, as he told the British ambassador, that he could "teach" the Mexicans "to elect good men." In a curious distortion of things, he persuaded himself that the diplomatic pressures he applied to Mexico, reinforced by the U.S. Navy in the Gulf of Mexico and U.S. Army on the border, represented a departure from the Latin American policies of his predecessors.

In other times, Wilson might not have been able to persevere with such a course, but the unsettled condition of Mexico—where revolutionary pretenders were also denouncing Huerta—and the prospect of conflict among European powers, which erupted in war in August 1914, played to his advantage. As the British grew more fearful of German ambitions on the Continent and in Latin America, they became more tolerant of Wilson's methods in Mexico. Certainly Germany in the Caribbean and Mexico was less a menace to Britain than to the United States, which had been suspicious of German designs in the New World since the 1902–3 Venezuelan crisis, but London had other reasons for accommodating a policy its diplomats believed futile if not naive. British acquiescence in his Mexican policy came after Wilson insisted that the United States must abide by a 1902 treaty pledging equal tolls for the shipping of all nations through the Panama Canal.[9]

In such a tense atmosphere, it is understandable how an ordinarily minor diplomatic incident could escalate into something more serious. In spring 1914 Huerta was besieged on every front: to the south lay Indian Mexico and the Zapatista rebellion against the hacienda, to the north the army of Pancho Villa, who was glorified by the socialist John Reed as the master strategist of guerrilla war, and yet another revolutionary pretender, Venustiano Carranza, who commanded the Constitutionalist army. Together with the menacing firepower of the U.S. naval vessels patrolling the Atlantic coast, this widespread revolt against Huerta signalled, inevitably, the dictator's collapse. But as the revolutionaries advanced against the dictator, Huerta was granted a momentary reprieve in his fall from grace. In April a Huertista officer in Tampico had arrested a party of seamen from the U.S.S. *Dolphin* who had come ashore for supplies and wandered into a restricted zone. They were ignominiously paraded through town. A superior quickly released them to their commander, Rear Adm. Henry Mayo.

Mayo was old-school Navy, whose officers were expected in critical situations to "use their best judgment" and take the consequences. Without consulting his commander, Mayo demanded a written apology, the hoisting of the U.S. flag in a prominent place in the city, and a 21-gun salute. By the time the demand filtered up through the respective bureaucracies, neither Wilson nor Huerta dared back down. Wilson thought the incident silly, and said so, but there were larger issues at stake, and when the Navy got word that a German ship was headed for Veracruz with arms for the beleaguered Huerta, the order came down to seize the port customshouse and intercept the arms. On 20 April, to the cheers of onlooking British seamen calling out, "Give 'em hell, Yanks!," naval landing craft maneuvered up to the docks of the city founded by Hernán Cortés in 1519. The officers who stepped ashore did not hear the cries of an American journalist who was rushing toward them, warning of snipers—prisoners released from jail by the retreating Mexican commander, given weapons, and told to defend the city. Three days later, after a devastating bombardment of the Mexican naval academy and house-to-house clearing of the snipers by U.S. Marines, Veracruz surrendered. The Americans counted 17 dead, the Mexicans at least 126 and possibly more, as the dead were ordered quickly interred by U.S. Authorities in the interest of public health. Some of the dead Mexicans were stacked, soaked with creosote, and publicly burned by American soldiers.

The Americans stayed in Veracruz for seven months and, under an Army command, gave the city, indisputably, the most honest governance in its history. Yet so bitterly resented was this invasion of Mexican soil that as late as 1952 the success of Mexican political candidates was threatened by accusations of abetting the U.S. military governors of the city in their youth. Wilson was shaken by news of the casualities and the accompanying hemispheric condemnation of the U.S. occupation. Equally troubling was the collective denunciation—save for Villa, who coveted U.S. approval—by Huerta's enemies, whose opposition to the occupation emboldened Huerta's cause and virtually foredoomed a hastily arranged peace conference urged by Argentina, Brazil, and Chile in Niagara Falls between American and Mexican negotiators. In the succeeding months Huerta's political strength quickly and decisively dissipated. In July 1914 he fled Mexico, and his relentless enemy, Venustiano Carranza, who had made no deal with the Americans, triumphantly entered the capital.[10]

Thus, Carranza benefitted by his opposition to Huerta and did not suffer from any concessions to the despised occupiers of Veracruz. Yet the victory of the Constitutionalists did not validate Wilson's policy toward revolutionary Mexico. As World War I and the issue of U.S. neutrality drew his attention to more serious confrontations on the high seas, the president increasingly viewed the continuing violence in Mexico in an international context. In the beginning, he had tried and failed to manipulate Huerta's opponents. Now that the revolutionary leaders had toppled the dictator, they could not agree among themselves. In late 1914 they gathered in Aguascalientes and defied the social conservative Carranza by adopting the agrarian reform platform of the Zapatistas. When Villa and Zapata allied their forces and drove Carranza from Mexico City, Wilson found himself in much the same predicament as his predecessor looking at the probable downfall of Díaz.

Carranza had an acute perception of the psychological toll the revolution was taking on the Mexican people and, more important, an uncanny instinct for sizing up Wilson's priorities. A country torn by war and revolutionary factions wanted a restoration of "legitimate" government; the American government, alert to German intriguing in northern Mexico, desperately wanted a secure neighbor. In 1915 Carranza set himself to deliver both. He issued tentative promises of agrarian reform as he dispatched yet another army into the North to crush his most formidable opponent, Villa. When Wilson declared that he was carefully weighing the Mexican situation and announced that he was seeking the advice of six other Latin American governments as to the "proper" leader of Mexico, Carranza correctly sensed that if he denounced this renewed threat of intervention and dealt with his opposition he would present Wilson and the world with a fait accompli. Carranza lobbied against Wilson's Pan American Pact as a yet another manifestation of U.S. interventionism. He persisted in his opposition to American meddling, and when 1915 ended, Woodrow Wilson, who for more than two years had tried to direct the course of Mexican revolution through political manipulation and even military intervention, recognized Venustiano Carranza as de facto president of Mexico.

Carranza had won the diplomatic battle but had not secured the volatile frontier. Mercenaries, socialists, and revolutionaries had warred for territory and influence along the border for five years. During the uncertain days before Carranza finally solidified his control over central Mexico, tales of German intrigue swept through dingy border towns. The most frightening was the Plan of San Diego, which called for an uprising of the Mexican population in the U.S. Southwest. Pancho Villa presented a more substantial threat. Once depicted as a hero by American journalists, Villa was now virtually isolated by the other Mexican revolutionary chieftains and abandoned by the U.S. government. Infuriated by the putative betrayal, he gathered a hundred or so faithful revolutionaries and commenced a private war. In January 1916 his soldiers stopped a train carrying American miners in Sonora and shot them. Two months later, the Villistas attacked the border town of Columbus, New Mexico.

The Columbus raid was yet another episode in what has been called the "secret war" in Mexico. One version held that German agents in northern Mexico, pretending to serve Villa's political ambitions, worked to bring about a U.S.–Mexican war; another presented the attack as a Villa tactic to prevent Carranza from accommodating the Americans and, in doing so, "selling out" the revolutionary cause. In either case, Wilson did not respond to the public cries for a full-scale invasion. Instead he responded to Carranza's order for Villa's apprehension by dispatching the Punitive Expedition under Brig. Gen. John J. Pershing to capture the Mexican bandit. Carranza swore to defend Mexican sovereignty and demanded that Pershing stay close to the border. When some of the American troops penetrated deep into Chihuahua, Carranza's soldiers fired on them.

There were renewed cries for a full-scale intervention, but with the likely U.S. involvement in the European war, Wilson could ill afford a worsening of the conflict with Mexico. Carranza had again outwitted his more powerful American counterpart. In late 1916, with a 10,000-man U.S. military force wandering in the Chihuahua vastness in a vain search for Pancho Villa, these two presidents warily followed the pronouncements of Mexico's Constitutional Congress that had convened at Querétaro. There, what both had long feared came about: radical spokesmen fought for and largely obtained a document that proclaimed as law the agrarian and social demands of the revolution. In a specific indictment of the foreign penetration of the nation, the framers of the Constitution of 1917 declared in Article 27 that the subsoil wealth of Mexico belonged to the nation and could not be alienated.

Most foreign entrepreneurs in Mexico were Americans, so the law directly affected Mexico's fragile diplomatic relations with the U.S. government. But instead of yielding to the pressures from without, Carranza accommodated the political realities from within. Again the deteriorating international scene benefitted him. In early 1917, anticipating war with Germany, Wilson ordered the last of American troops out of Mexico. In February the British released to the American government the contents of the Zimmermann telegram, a secret message to the German ambassador in Mexico that the British had intercepted and decoded. This revelation of Germany's plot to involve Mexico in its war with the United States presented Wilson with another difficult choice. If he challenged the Mexican government over the Zimmermann telegram and the constitutional decrees—which, it can be argued, fulfilled Wilson's call in 1914 for political and social justice in revolutionary Mexico—he ran the risk of driving Carranza into the German camp.

When the United States entered the European war in April 1917, its relations with Mexico were still tense. But the fear of the British and French that their American ally would be driven into a second Mexican war by German promises and intrigue did not come about. Carranza was undoubtedly pro-German in the war, but he did not succumb to German diplomatic pressure and renounce Mexican neutrality. The Mexican revolutionaries had defied Wilson's determined efforts to "guide" them and in 1917 had proclaimed what many Americans considered a socialist constitution. Although the revolutionaries' resistance had befuddled and angered the U.S. government, the Mexicans' historic tendency to resist the foreign intruder whether he comes to do ill or good unintentionally served U.S. wartime interests. Germany, if victorious, had pledged in the Zimmermann telegram to reward its Mexican ally with a return of the U.S. Southwest. If Mexico had joined Germany in the war, a force much larger than the Punitive Expedition would have been sent to the border and the American Expeditionary Force dispatched to the more critical European theater would have been weakened. Quite unintentionally, Carranza and Wilson, in their calculating restraint, abetted mutual causes.[11]

With the American government preoccupied with the European war, Carranza now set himself to establishing political control of Mexico. Here he benefitted from the decision of the revolutionaries who had crafted the 1917 Constitution to accept the Porifirian tradition of a domineering state. With the authoritative use of power he hounded his revolutionary rivals. In the North, the Villistas disbanded to avoid a confrontation with Carranza's armies; in the South, in Indian Mexico, a Carrancista officer lured Zapata into an ambush and killed him. A brief crisis occurred in 1918 and 1919 when U.S. State Department hardliners, responding to complaints from oil companies protesting higher taxes and calls for intervention from southwestern political leaders, pushed for a showdown. But Carranza weathered the crisis by persuading the U.S. government that Article 27 did not mean confiscation of oil properties. The last U.S. incursion into Mexico occurred in June 1919, when Villa, who had put together a band of disgruntled anti-Carrancistas, attacked Ciudad Juárez. When the Mexican federals proved unable to run him off, a U.S. military force crossed the Rio Grande and drove him away.

For all his efforts, Woodrow Wilson was unable to manipulate the twentieth century's first modern revolution, nor did the persistent U.S. diplomatic pressures and military intrusions deter a generation of Mexican revolutionary leaders from defining that revolution. Warring among themselves over territory and influence, they united to produce a document—the 1917 Constitution—that was distinctively Mexican, a curious blend of nineteenth-century liberalism in its exaltation of anticlericalism and of modern reformism in its affirmation of social justice. Western Europe and the United States viewed the carnage and human despair wrought by the revolution with disbelief and, in the U.S. Southwest, with justifiable fear that the violence would spill over the border. Wilson managed to keep the revolution within Mexican boundaries but, despite his benevolent professions and understanding, did little to shape its course. Yet he restrained more belligerent voices within his government who sought to crush the revolution, and his restraint meant that the U.S.–Mexican relationship would take on a new, albeit uncertain, character.

The surviving revolutionaries showed the world that their cause had been driven by forces within Mexico but had yet to demonstrate what kind of Mexico they intended to bring about. There were still many claimants to Porfirio Díaz's presidential chair, and in 1920, when Carranza tried to name his successor, his former revolutionary allies, led by Alvaro Obregón, drove him from office. He was waylaid along the route to Veracruz, taken to a country hut, and shot, it was said, at Obregón's order. Obregón took his prize of victory by occupying the national palace and petitioning Washington for recognition, only to receive yet another U.S. protest over the oil question in reply. Over the next few years the harassed Obregón fended off American demands for a treaty and simultaneously tried to persuade Mexicans that he was not compromising national sovereignty by pressing Mexican courts to render decisions favorable to U.S. oil companies. After U.S. businesses with interests in Mexico indicated they were willing to operate in a revolutionary state, the State Department ceased its diplomatic wrangling over the legitimacy of Obregón's government. In a series of conferences in 1923, the two countries thrashed out the Bucareli agreement, under which the Mexicans agreed to pay cash for any expropriated property greater than 4,400 acres, and the Americans to accept Mexican bonds for expropriations of smaller acreage. On the thorny issue of petroleum, already the symbol of revolutionary nationalism, the Mexicans promised only to refrain from enforcing Article 27 if the drillers performed "positive acts" of developing their leases. The agreement came just in time for Obregón: with it he got diplomatic recognition and desperately needed arms to crush a revolt against him.[12] It was the first step in a 20-year period of difficult readjustment between the two nations.

The 1920s were stormy years in the official relationship. American business, not yet adjusted to the revolutionary political tremors, expected its government to revive pre-revolutionary diplomatic styles in dealing with successive Mexican leaders. Ultimately, Washington and U.S. business slowly began to accommodate the new Mexico. After the civil war of 1923–24, which rose out of the competition of former generals for the presidency, Obregón virtually handpicked his successor, Plutarco Elías Calles. The new leader began to corral his rivals and lay the foundation of a national political party. Foreigners, the church, and, increasingly, the discontented revolutionary generals scattered in governorships and sinecures throughout the republic now felt the authoritative reach of the leader of the revolutionary state. Calles enforced anticlerical laws, applauded labor unions, and advanced the cause of agrarian reform. Foreign oil companies, the putative beneficiaries of the Bucareli agreement, were again thrown into uncertainty as Callista judges began handling down decrees against them.

By mid-decade the U.S. secretary of state and congressmen from the Southwest were regularly denoucing the new regime as socialist. Cries of Bolshevik Mexico rang out on Capitol Hill. After one of Calles's anti-American decrees, President Calvin Coolidge, in unusually denunciatory words, declared that "Mexico was on trial before the world." In what would be standard procedure in future diplomatic confrontations, Calles hired an American pamphleteer and translator who collected his various decrees and published them under the title "Mexico on Trial before the World." In actuality, the U.S. government and press had failed to look beyond the militant rhetoric coming out of Mexico. Undeniably, the tentative Mexican involvement in the Nicaraguan civil war of 1926–27 and the sanctuary the Mexican government provided Augusto C. Sandino, the military leader of the anti-American guerrilla army in Nicaragua, exacerbated the oil controversy. But had American political leaders examined more closely the internal dynamics of Calles's governance, they would have recognized a crafty revolutionary disciple building a power base, co-opting potential labor troublemakers, and extending the power of the state into the countryside.

Fortunately, Coolidge, responding to conciliatory elements in the U.S. business community, had the good sense to assess the economic cost of the diplomatic confrontation with Calles. He called back the vocal U.S. ambassador, James Sheffield, and sent in his place Dwight Morrow, who proceeded to charm the initially suspicious Mexicans. Accustomed to Yankees who patronized, Calles now confronted a likable American who made no pretense of trying to understand Mexico and Mexicans or "guide" them but simply professed to "like" them. In a short time, Morrow was meeting privately with the *jefe máximo* ("maximum chief") in the president's country villa and discussing everything from the oil dispute to clerical issues and political economics. Before long Mexican judges were abruptly reversing their predecessors' decisions against U.S. oil concerns. From the Mexican presidential palace came a series of pronouncements speedily formalized into regulations governing their future. Clearly, despite their antiforeign rhetoric, this wave of revolutionary leaders intended to keep Mexico in the orbit of world capitalism, which meant maintaining links to the U.S. economy.

As the oil imbroglio abated, Morrow threw his energies into reconciling church and state in the volatile Mexican countryside, where a generation of inspired revolutionary schoolteachers, dispatched by education czar José Vasconcelos, were at war, the *cristero* revolt, with country priests, who denounced them as the devil's disciples. Mexico's bishops had condemned the secularization of education and urged resistance of the government order that priests register with federal authorities and then shut down the churches. Calles retaliated by calling for new anticlerical laws. Morrow interceded, persuading Calles to meet secretly with a liberal American Catholic priest, John J. Burke, who worked out an arrangement between the government and the bishops. Calles eased the pressure and the churches reopened, but the anticlerical laws remained.

By then Calles had vacated the presidential palace but had not left politics. The return to power of President-elect Obregón was thwarted when Calles's former mentor was assassinated by a Catholic zealot in 1928. Calles then assumed the role of *jefe político* (political boss). For another six years he "managed" the presidency, heavily influencing the three *políticos* (Emilio Portes Gil, Pascual Ortiz Rubio, and Abelardo Rodríguez) who entered and then hastily exited the presidential palace. Calles's legacy to Depression-era Mexico was a six-year plan inspired by but less severe than the Soviet model; the ruling Partido Nacional Revolucionario, later to evolve into the Partido Revolucionario Institucional (PRI); and a slowing of the agrarian reform. In what proved to be his final exercise of presidential selection in 1934, Calles chose Lázaro Cárdenas of Michoacán. The revolution, Calles believed, had run its leftist course.

Calles's assessment of the revolution was premature, however, for within two years he was in exile, and Cárdenas was busily reordering the revolutionary agenda in the service of the state and the revolutionary party. Despite its challenge to U.S. power, the revolution modified the rules but had not broken the bonds with the U.S. economy. Sixty percent of Mexican exports in 1930 (as hemispheric trade began to shrink under the burden of the Depression) went north; 70 percent of Mexican imports came from the United States. Along the northern border once isolated Mexican villages had grown into a service economy (of women and liquor) for the Anglos on the other side.

The Depression in the United States ultimately spread into Mexico. Three hundred thousand Mexicans returned to a nation where the revolutionary promise to *los de abajo* (those from below) was not yet fulfilled. Anti-American protests racked Mexican cities, and a series of strikes erupted in the foreign-owned oil companies, where workers were bitter about unresolved labor problems and angry at the United States' deportation of Mexicans whose labor was no longer needed north of the border. Pressed from above and pushed from below, Cárdenas responded in a manner that his successors would often emulate: he used the power of a state to confront social issues, not with any realistic hope of resolving them but with the certainty that any Mexican president who does not respond to the rumblings from below will inevitably be swept away by them.

The new *jefe máximo* had a pronounced populist style. He revived agrarian reform, embraced labor and its cause, and, just as the first generation of postrevolutionary Mexican leaders, alarmed the foreign community and the landowners who had managed to survive three decades of agrarian reform. There was renewed fears of a socialist Mexico and, as in the 1920s, a worsening of tensions with the U.S. government. The image of revolutionary Mexico in that decade had confused American onlookers. Now Cárdenas's enthusiasm for social and economic justice—a fulfillment of the revolutionary promise to the majority of Mexicans who remained propertyless—distracted Americans from assessing the more lasting consequences of his policies.

The revolutionary now charting Mexico's future confronted a dual challenge. The first was the return of migrant workers who had gone north to labor in industrial America in the 1920s and had been deported by the U.S. government with the collapse of its economy. Mexico received its returning children, but Cárdenas knew their presence in the countryside, which the revolution had scarcely changed, exacerbated the social problem. If Mexico wanted to feed its people, it made no sense to break up the old landowning system. But to delay the breakup threatened the government's plan to extend the political reach of the state into rural areas. Cárdenas recognized that the revolution had sprung up from the countryside and could be brought down by the counterrevolution that was taking shape there in the alliance of landowners, church, and small farmers.

Political survival was the second challenge, which dictated a resolution of the agrarian issue via the exercise of state power, even in defiance of economic logic. As long as Mexican labor and Mexican and American capital were tied to the land, landowners would dictate the character of the social order and in turn the political reality of the countryside. The solution was the confiscation and dispensation of land to villages to hold in common or in enormous amounts, as in the Laguna cotton district in Durango-Coahuila, where 30,000 families farmed a giant cooperative. The revival of the agrarian question signalled an abrupt turn in the course of the revolution, but it was a necessary step for the revolution's survival and for Mexico's impressive economic development in the postwar era.[13]

TWO ECONOMIES: THE POSTWAR RELATIONSHIP

After World War II Lázaro Cárdenas emerged as the heroic revolutionary leader who had battled for social justice. He had responded to lingering popular causes with the agrarian reform program that restructured rural Mexico and by fashioning a new political culture founded on mass organizations, especially labor. When he assumed power in 1934, labor had not yet been incorporated fully into the revolutionary political culture. Cárdenas's determination to do so set the revolution on collision course with the international economic order and brought Mexico into yet another confrontation with the United States.

Nowhere was the confrontation more dramatic, nor more symbolic of Mexican revolutionary nationalism, than in the oil expropriation crisis of 1938, which occurred amidst the global threat of fascism and the ongoing debate in Latin America between economic statism and democratic capitalism. Franklin D. Roosevelt, bent on constructing a hemispheric antifascist coalition to satisfy U.S. strategic interests, was alert to the political implications of Cárdenas's revival of revolutionary xenophobia. Roosevelt dispatched former Secretary of the Navy Josephus Daniels to Mexico City to reassure Cárdenas that the New Deal and the revolution were kindred spirits in their responsiveness to social issues. A decade before, Ambassador Dwight Morrow and President Calles had developed a mutually beneficial relationship. Morrow had discarded the patronizing approach of his predecessor for a more congenial diplomatic style, and Calles had followed with declarations that placated foreign investors. But what Morrow had overlooked and Roosevelt did not acutely perceive was that the understanding between Calles and

Morrow had been possible because *Calles* had chosen to maintain Mexico's place in the international economic order. This was not Cárdenas's first priority.

Daniels generally accepted the leftward drift of the revolution. When Cárdenas announced the expropriation of both Mexican- and American-owned lands, Daniels politely acquiesced, saying only that prompt compensation should be made in bonds. Cárdenas demurred, and in 1937 the Mexican government undertook a massive expropriation in the Yaqui Valley in Sonora that affected both American and Mexican holdings. Again, Daniels was noticeably restrained. But when in the following year Cárdenas issued an executive order nationalizing foreign oil concerns, it was clear that he went too far for even the tolerant Daniels, who was unable to placate infuriated oil cartel moguls.

The oil imbroglio, which went back to the disputes of the 1920s over the application of Article 27 of the 1917 Constitution, had begun to worsen in 1936 with legislation in the Mexican Congress permitting the government to seize private property in the public interest and defer compensation for 10 years. As the Depression set in, Mexico, like other Latin American governments, declared a moratorium on its international obligations, but under Cárdenas Mexico went further in encouraging confrontations with foreign interests. Labor unions, especially in the petroleum industry, were emboldened by pro-labor decrees. They formed a united front and presented the oil companies with a list of demands that amounted to 65 million pesos in increased wages and employee benefits. The companies responded with an offer of 14 million. Cárdenas's agents made a fitful effort to mediate, but the talks fell through, and the companies began digging in for a long fight. As expected, the workers struck in May 1937, and Cárdenas again interceded. This time, however, his intention was not to resolve the strike but to obtain vital information about the companies' ability to meet union demands. Convinced that the oil triumvirate of U.S., British, and Dutch concerns could pay more than their original offer without bankruptcy, Cárdenas pressed both labor and management to accept a 26 million peso settlement. The unions agreed, but the companies refused and looked to their governments for support. Although the triumvirate's directors had vowed to fight, only the U.S. government dared confront the Mexicans on this issue.

It was matter of factly presumed that the crisis would result in a government takeover of oil operations but only a *temporary* one, for the move would precipitate a harsh diplomatic note from Washington to which Mexico would quickly acquiesce. In early March 1938 the Mexican Supreme Court handed down a judgment against the companies, which appeared ready to capitulate by mid-month. But neither the company managers nor even the nominally attentive Daniels anticipated Cárdenas's dramatic 18 March announcement that *all* foreign petroleum holdings in Mexico would be nationalized. Roosevelt was taken aback. He had been making the obligatory gestures to hemispheric nationalism in order to advance the anti-German coalition. Now he faced in Cárdenas's Mexico a threat to U.S. credibility. The State Department announced that Mexico of course had a sovereign right to nationalize the companies but must offer immediate compensation.

Cárdenas refused. Washington pressed for arbitration, and again Cárdenas rejected the offer. Cárdenas was confronted with yet another upheaval in rural Mexico—the Sinarquista rebellion, in which capitalists, conservative landowners, and the church joined ranks against the revolution—and moved to crush it, but he did not back off from the international battle over Mexican petroleum. The oil companies, alert to the implications this dispute might have for their position in Venezuela, wanted to avoid being symbolically defeated by a government they had once been able to intimidate. But in Washington and London, officials were already calculating the strategic ramifications of the crisis. As the conflict with Mexico had undermined Woodrow Wilson's Pan American Pact in 1916, Mexican revolutionary nationalism threatened Roosevelt's hemispheric defense strategy.

In the uncertainty, Cárdenas moved decisively. He created PEMEX (the Mexican Petroleum Company), found a renegade U.S. oil company willing to defy Washington and supply the Mexicans with the equipment to operate it, and, when the Americans and British refused to buy PEMEX oil, began selling it to the Germans. By 1940, when Cárdenas left office, the oil crisis had largely passed, though the companies continued with their protests for several years. Ultimately, the companies were compensated, but by the Mexican calculation of the worth of their holdings. And often they were paid in part with small donations of a few pesos or a ring or something of value from ordinary Mexicans who wished to tell the world that the oil beneath the ground in their country belonged to Mexico and its people.[1]

A decade earlier, the United States would not have yielded so readily to Mexican defiance, but in summer 1940 the Roosevelt administration desperately needed Mexican support in its efforts to create a hemispheric alliance against the Axis powers of Germany, Italy, and Japan. At the eighth Inter-American conference in Lima in 1938, Mexico and Argentina were the most outspoken in their defense of absolute nonintervention and were noticeably reluctant to join Secretary of State Cordell Hull in condemning the German economic and political involvement in Latin America. Argentina's vulnerability to German pressure was understandable if irritating, but Mexican neutrality in the approaching global struggle was intolerable. Mexico had strategic materials—particularly oil—that were vital to U.S. defense interests.

During World War I the United States had effectively undermined German strategy in revolutionary Mexico with a combination of diplomatic, economic, and military pressures. Confronting a still defiant Mexican state in 1940, the United States now chose the more prudent course of negotiation and accommodation. The petroleum and agrarian expropriation squabbles rapidly diminished in importance for both governments, but for different reasons. For Washington, their resolution in the United States' favor was less critical than a friendly and cooperative Mexico in the unstable international arena. For Mexico City, their expeditious settlement gave Cárdenas and his chosen successor, Manuel Avila Camacho, the opportunity to direct their energies to the Sinarquista rebellion in rural Mexico. An antirevolutionary union of conservative businessmen, the church, and small landowners presented a growing political threat to the revolutionary state. The putative leader of the rebellion was the Indian governor of San Luis Potosí, Saturnino Cedillo, himself a former revolutionary. Cedillo's revolt was crushed, but his followers founded a new party, Partido Acción Nacional (PAN), and fielded a candidate in the 1940 election. For a few months there circulated rumors that the PAN candidate, if able to raise an army and gain control of several Mexican states, would be recognized by the United States as the legitimate president of the country.

But Roosevelt provided no encouragement to the plotters, and Cárdenas alertly stationed Mexican troops in some of the more volatile political states. Avila Camacho, supported by Cárdenas, was swept into office in one of the most fraudulent elections in modern Mexican history, but the presence of Vice-President-elect Henry Wallace at his inauguration confirmed what generations of Mexican *políticos* have believed: when the U.S. government has to choose between principle and national interest, it will choose the latter. In the precarious circumstances of the day, it made the correct choice. Avila Camacho was pro-business, pro-American, and a professing Catholic. He condemned fascism, closed down pro-German clubs, and blacklisted German firms in Mexico. When the German ambassador accused him of being a lackey of the Yankees, Avila Camacho reprimanded him by declaring that Mexico would follow the dictation of no government in its internal affairs. The German attack on the Soviet Union in June 1941, which roused the Mexican Left in support of the government's anti-German policies, prompted Mexico to sever economic ties with Germany and crack down on pro-German elements in the country.

To Washington, such dramatic shifts in Mexican foreign policy were heartening but did not signal a sea change in Mexican thinking. They represented, frankly, an adjustment to international realities. The Mexican Left openly called for a "second front" against the Axis, but its vocal belligerence obscured a divided and, in rural areas, disinterested Mexican populace. Yet Avila Camacho remained alert to the shifting political winds in both countries. The campaign against the Sinarquistas and especially the government's cracking down on German business and social organizations, predictably, had infuriated the pro-German elements in the United States. Father Charles Coughlin, the Detroit radio priest who had been denouncing FDR's New Deal, now condemned the Mexicans for allowing the Comintern to enter Mexico and "Sovietize" the country. But the newspapers of mainstream America lauded Avila Camacho's leadership and praised Mexico for its political and economic advancements.[2]

The day after the Japanese bombed Pearl Harbor, Mexico dutifully broke relations with Japan but did not join with the United States in declaring war. A few weeks later, grim reports in the newspaper El Universal told of hoarding by food suppliers in an effort by Nazi fifth columnists and their Spanish allies to frighten poor Mexicans over the nation's possible involvement in a U.S. war against Germany. The government's response was to crack down even harder against German nationals, a campaign facilitated with timely information on German espionage from the U.S. State Department. Yet the Mexican president was cautious about Mexico's priorities in the international crisis. In his New Year's Day address, Avila Camacho solemnly declared that Mexico's contribution to the global struggle would be in production in industry and agriculture. In a special memorandum on outstanding political issues with the United States—the agrarian and petroleum settlements, which exacerbated the nation's debt problem, and the Mexican–American Commission of Continental Defense—he noted that Mexico should demonstrate "full cooperation" with Washington.[3]

Two years before, such a statement would have been unthinkable for any Mexican president. Anti-Americanism still ran deep in Mexico, and Mexican leaders retained their inherited suspicions of a malevolent and interventionist United States, but Cárdenas had demonstrated that, in defiance, Mexico could earn the United States' respect. That victory achieved, Avila Camacho had no intention of making Carranza's error by cultivating the enemies of the United States. The government's internal enemies were pro-Axis. Its planners anticipated Mexico's inevitable absorption into the international capitalist order of the United States, not Germany. To Washington, Avila Camacho dispatched his unrepentantly pro-American foreign minister, Ezequiel Padilla, who echoed Avila Camacho's anti-German sentiments in public addresses. Aging Mexican políticos, recalling the anti-Americanism of the revolution and Carranza's denunciation of Woodrow Wilson's 1916 Pan American Pact, were taken aback, but Avila Camacho's pronouncements were aimed at placating the United States (increasingly dependent on Mexican petroleum for its industrial mobilization) and, more important, reminding the vocal pro-German crowd within Mexico of its uncertain political future.

But not even the shrewd Avila Camacho could mollify Adolf Hitler, whose submarine commanders had been intercepting Mexican ships and warning their captains of the "grave risk" if Mexico persisted in supplying the Americans with petroleum. In May 1942 German U-boats sank two Mexican tankers. Twelve Mexicans died. Throughout the country the Germans were denounced, but, surprisingly, only the Left and government workers favored a declaration of war. At first, Avila Camacho was content with a formal protest to Berlin. When the Germans did not make a satisfactory response, he called his cabinet, the Congress, and state governors to the capital. On 30 May Mexico formally declared war on the Axis powers. Simultaneously, the Mexican congress made Avila Camacho the "virtual dictator" of the nation. Mexico, the president told the nation a few days later, had no choice. The response of Germany, Japan, and Italy to the government's protests of violations of Mexican neutrality had "not only demonstrated their customary discourtesy but tacitly admitted their material and moral responsibility for the sinking."[4]

Although the prospect of aiding the gringos was repugnant to many Mexicans, they supported the president's decision for patriotic reasons. Throughout the nation there was a call for unity in support of the war effort. The heavily politicized labor unions, divided by factional disputes, were bound into a coalition under the firm control of the state. In a major pact with the U.S. government, Mexico agreed to supply farm workers (braceros) to American growers, largely in the Southwest. The Mexican government was thus provided an opportunity to reduce the rural areas of west-central Mexico, where the Sinarquista movement had been strong, of independent farmers and politically hostile campesinos. The government created a Supreme Defense Council, bringing together representatives of the "cooperative" sectors of society with the usually disputatious middle class, and called on Mexicans to restrain their demands for consumer goods in the interests of production for the global struggle. Like Americans, Mexicans were expected to sacrifice, and they did. They participated in blackouts, civil defense exercises, and, like Americans, tolerated an ever-burgeoning bureaucracy with its predictably stupid and mindless regulations. In 1942 Avila Camacho chose Mexican Independence Day, 16 September, ordinarily dedicated to celebrations and patrotic addresses, to commit his presidency to national reconciliation. At his side, linking arms, were six ex-presidents of Mexico.

Most Americans, recalling only the bracero agreement and the air squadron dispatched to the Philippines, denigrate Mexico's participation in World War II, but the Mexican role was consequential. Mexico supplied strategic materials (oil, zinc, mercury, cadmium, copper, lead, henequen, sisal, and antimony), food, and especially labor for the United States' farms, railroads, and war plants. Two hundred fifty thousand Mexicans in the United States— many subject to conscription—served in the U.S. military, 14,000 of them in a war theater. A Mexican astrophysicist was part of the team in Los Alamos, New Mexico, that developed the atomic bomb.

On the political level, Mexico joined the United Nations and committed itself to a war for democracy. In April 1943, in a meeting with Avila Camacho in Monterrey (the first official visit of a U.S. president to Mexico), Roosevelt declared that the "exploitation of resources and people by one country for the benefit of another has definitely passed." Heartened by this reaffirmation of the Good Neighbor policy, Avila Camacho traveled on FDR's presidential train to Corpus Christi, Texas. En route, these two executives with different political agendas and certainly different political styles, fashioned a wartime understanding that linked Mexico's economic future with that of its northern neighbor.

This was not the goal of either government. Wartime patterns rather accidentally became peacetime economic realities. Such organizations as the Joint Defense Committee—which coordinated U.S. Army plans for the Southwest with the Mexican Pacific coast command, trained Mexican officers at U.S. installations, and helped the Mexicans modernize their military—barely survived the war. By 1946 the Mexicans, for political reasons, were resisting U.S. pressures to involve the country in continental defense schemes. But the necessities of war created economic bonds that could not be easily severed. True, the Mexican railway laborers could be repatriated to make room for returning soldiers, but American farmers—especially in the Southwest, where a battle between agro-business and farm unions threatened—looked on the braceros as vital to their interests. Inspired by the vigorous expansion of manufacturing and exports during the war, Mexico desperately needed these people for its domestic labor force. Mexico lacked sufficient capital goods for emulating the industrial giant to the north, but with its people, resources, and leaders who spoke of an "institutional revolution," it appeared that the country would be modernized. Cárdenas's vision of an independent nation, poor but self-sufficient, now dissipated in fanciful talk of a modern industrial one. Such a Mexico could afford to be politically but not economically defiant of the United States.[5]

At the "Conference on The Problems of War and Peace," which convened at Chapúltepec to confront postwar economic issues and the troublesome question of Argentina's admission into the United Nations, Mexico occupied a centrally important diplomatic position. From the beginning of the war, the Argentines had resisted U.S. efforts to bend them to Washington's hemispheric will. For a few years, Argentina's putatively pro-German leaders had managed to frustrate American diplomacy in neighboring countries, but one by one the other Southern Cone nations had fallen into line. By the end of 1944 even Argentina's military chieftains—including Juan Domingo Perón, who benefitted politically in the subsequent confrontation with the Yankees—were ready to negotiate with the furious Americans. Yet most Latin American leaders instinctively understood the Argentine position.

The Mexicans, who had frustrated Wilsonian Pan Americanism a generation before, now saw themselves as mediators between the repentant Argentines and the sulking Americans, who sought a unified hemisphere at their beck and call but did not want the diplomatic indignity of caving in to the Argentines. For Foreign Minister Padilla, who spoke of a Western Hemisphere with a "new destiny . . . [and] united against adversity," the Argentine squabble was an opportunity not only to reconcile two warring hemispheric republics but to enhance his political prospects for the 1946 Mexican presidential election. Padilla was hated by both Mexico's Right and Left. He had prosecuted the Catholic fanatic who had assissinated Obregón in 1928 and was generally viewed by rightists, who called him "the Frog," as a tool of American designs in Mexico. Leftist opposition, directed principally by the powerful labor leader Vicente Lombardo Toledano and former President Cárdenas, had developed quickly when the Soviet government had denounced the Argentines for their complicity with the Axis.[6] Padilla spoke disdainfully of Mexican labor's noticeable postwar shift to the left on international questions.

For Latin America and especially for Mexico, the critical issue was postwar economic development. For the United States, a related but more important matter was which political strategy Latin America's postwar leaders—most of them vulnerable to powerful social forces generated by the wartime denial of consumer goods—would follow to modernize their economies. Mexico's choices were particularly critical, but among the U.S. diplomats and technicians who served in Mexico during the war and witnessed the country's impressive economic alteration, there was little doubt about the nation's industrial future. Denied by war's curtailments the goods and equipment they had once imported, the Mexicans had expanded manufacturing, begun exporting north, and whetted domestic appetites for consumer goods. The loss of the U.S. market in the postwar adjustment was inevitable. The Mexicans wanted to protect the national economy from American imports and build up their own. A few sympathetic bureaucrats in the State Department argued that the United States had a profound obligation to Mexico (and indeed to Latin America) for wartime sacrifices and thus it should be given special consideration for economic assistance, technology, and credit. Merwin Bohan, a technical officer of the U.S. delegation at Chapúltepec, expressed this sentiment when he wrote, "Our war-acquired obligations cannot be fully liquidated by maintaining that the cash we paid for their goods, the sacrifices we made in furnishing them with supplies, and protection given by our armed forces constitute payment in full. . . . Latin America, despite the scoffers and the cynics, has contributed something more to the common effort than material things."[7]

But already the U.S. global vision was shifting from a north-south to an east-west angle, which augured well for Western Europe but meant that many of Latin America's wartime economic gains would be lost in the peacetime adjustment. Mexico was especially vulnerable. In the war it had exported much, imported little; in the process it had built up impressive amounts of foreign exchange. But the inevitable inflationary spiral of too much money chasing too few goods was followed at war's end by too many imports at higher prices and the unpleasant prospect that the country (as much of Latin America) would again lapse into indebtedness and reassume its role as supplier of raw materials.

To the Mexican Left, this meant economic dependence and neocolonialism and explains much about the political turbulence within the revolutionary family at war's end and why Roosevelt and especially Truman viewed

Mexico as something of a test case for their global strategies. The United States could tolerate a Mexico that departed or publicly disagreed with its cold war foreign policy agenda, but the U.S. economy, at home and abroad, could not adjust to a socialist Mexico with a government intent on fulfilling the revolutionary vision. For this reason, George Messersmith, FDR's ambassador to Mexico in 1945, cultivated such politically ambitious men as Padilla, who had apparently convinced Messersmith that the Mexicans wished "to keep their thinking [on postwar economic problems] in line with ours" and would resist the economic philosophy of protectionism Latin American leaders were advocating.[8]

But Mexican *políticos* have a way of accommodating U.S. economic priorities without following Washington's political guidance. As soon as Avila Camacho and the revolutionary chieftains discovered that Padilla was the American choice as his successor, they immediately found their own candidate, Miguel Alemán, the president's secretary of the interior (Gobernación), after the president the most powerful official in the Mexican government. The unofficial view of Alemán circulating in the State Department ranged from "obstructive," anti-American, and devious to "smart" and "willing to play ball" with the United States. Messersmith was suspicious of Alemán and made his views known in Washington. But John Carrigan of the Division of Mexican Affairs proved the most perceptive with his observation that Padilla would be a risk precisely because he was popular with Americans and unpopular with Mexicans and, if victorious, could ill afford to favor U.S. interests.[9] With that admonition, Messersmith's hostility subsided, though when Alemán visited San Antonio, Texas, with Cantinflas, the famous Mexican comic, to raise money for his campaign Messersmith properly complained.

Alemán promptly declared that neither the U.S. government nor the Mexican military would interfere in the electoral process; privately assured the U.S. embassy that he would not appoint a Communist to his cabinet; pledged to industrialize Mexico; changed the name of the official party to Partido Revolucionario Institutional (PRI) and its theme from a "Democracy of Workers" to "Democracy and Social Justice"; and reassured the business sector that it had a place in Mexico's economic future.[10]

Messersmith's concerns—that Alemán's election would advance Soviet ambitions in Mexico—should be measured along with the contemporaneous efforts of Ambassador Spruille Braden to deny Juan Perón the presidency of Argentina. Like his kindred spirit in Buenos Aires, Messersmith misinterpreted the domestic political protest against government candidates as a signal for the United States to act, not by intervening but, as the ambassador expressed, to reassure "thoughtful people" in Mexico by making "our principles clear."[11] But even the suspicious Messersmith clearly saw that Alemán would need U.S. assistance to modernize the Mexican economy. The dependent links forged in the war could not be readily undone. To be sure, Mexican manufacturing and industry had achieved much but had done so at the expense of food production. In early 1946 there were fears that the United States intended no longer to supply the grains it had during the war. This was a rumor that Messersmith immediately denied with fulsome reassurances to the Mexicans that the nation's grain shipments would be continued. The political implications of food shortages in Mexico, he told President Harry Truman, left the United States with no other choice: "There would be a revolution and the red flag in Mexico within three months if its wheat needs are not met."[12]

His reasoning was yet another sign that Mexico occupied a critical place in the evolving U.S. policy toward Latin America. Mexico's political and social stability—and its economic modernization within the expanding U.S. international economy—offered a persuasive example to post-World War II Pan Americanists. Most Pan Americanists were critical of U.S. interventionism in hemispheric affairs but championed the Latin American case for economic assistance. When the United States announced the Marshall Plan for Europe in 1948, Pan Americanists sought a similar measure for the Western Hemisphere. If denied, the argument went, hemispheric governments would look beyond the United States (as they had done in the 1930s) for their economic models. This was a simplistic logic ultimately rejected by representatives (and by George C. Marshall himself) at Pan hemispheric conferences in Rio de Janeiro in 1947 and Bogotá in 1948. At those conferences the hemispheric governments fashioned, respectively, the Inter-American Treaty of Reciprocal Assistance and the Organization of American States. The high-level economic conference sought by the Latin American signatories did not convene for almost a decade and the "Marshall Plan" for Latin America, the Alliance for Progress, was not developed until 1961. Truman himself was typically blunt about Europe's and Latin America's comparative economic needs: "The problems of countries in this Hemisphere are different in nature and cannot be relieved by the same means and the same approaches."[13]

Such a philosophy more or less reflected the political strategy of the "institutionalized" revolution. Alemán and his generation either co-opted or defused their opposition. Business—even foreign-owned business—had a future in Mexico if it subsumed its politics in the new order or, in the words of Mexican politicians, in the harmony of the new era. Small businessmen and shopkeepers found a place in the "public" sector of the national party; big business, identified in Mexico with the major concerns of Monterrey, "Mexico's Pittsburgh," acquiesced in political reality by accepting state direction in national development. In the volatile labor sector, the government simply used its political clout and, with the untimely death in 1945 of Soviet ambassador Constantin Oumansky, who since his arrival had proselytized the Soviet model, defanged opposition leader Lombardo Toledano. Within a year after taking office, Alemán had, through guile, tact, and effective use of the considerable power at the disposal of Mexican presidents, subordinated the state and, presumably, all Mexico to his bidding.

Every sector felt the reach of the state, all benefitted, but some did better than others. The revolution had finally rid rural Mexico of most foreign landowners, but in the modern Mexico that came to fruition after World War II the large *Mexican* producer, if politically subservient, thrived, especially in the Northwest, where Avila Camacho had initiated ambitous irrigation projects to reclaim largely unproductive lands. A parallel expansion of Mexican transportation and communication, especially into hitherto isolated rural areas, benefitted all rural Mexicans but helped the large agricultural producers more than the campesino. Cárdenas had restored the campesino to center stage in his rural strategy; under Avila Camacho and especially under Alemán, the government continued the *ejido* (communal landholding) program, but the program became increasingly peripheral simply because communal holdings were less productive than the private agricultural sector. Industry (steel, cement, paper, chemicals) was favored over agriculture, the irrigated agro-export sector of large irrigated farms over the rain-fed small farms of central Mexico.

Those who criticize this fundamentally political decision, as does James Cockcroft in a Marxist analysis of the Mexican economy from colonial times, indict Alemán not only for the social calamities that later plagued Mexico but also for a betrayal of the Mexican revolution.[14] Forgetting their pledge to create a more just social order, especially in the countryside, Mexico's leaders after Cárdenas used their political power to advance the interests of urban over rural Mexico, of large business over labor, and (when it proved cooperative) of foreign capital over the small but ambitious Mexican entrepreneur. These leaders did not abandon Cárdenas's dream but remembered the lessons and especially the opportunities of Mexico's wartime economic experience. Shielded by protectionist economic policies, Mexican manufacturers, with their politically docile labor force, dispensed shoddily made goods for the expanding internal market. Faced with an industrializing economy, the middle class had sufficient resources to purchase foreign-made items that suited its consumer preferences, and Alemán made certain that industry, sorely lacking in capital goods, had easier access to credit and less burdensome import duties. Foreign investment, which had diminished severely in the 1920s and especially the 1930s, now reappeared but not in railroads, utilities, government bonds, or the extractive industries. Instead it joined with Mexican capitalists, most of whom had made their money in the overheated wartime economy, in new enterprises geared to the expanding consumer market. In doing so, of course, foreign investors took a less hostile view of the intrusion of the Mexican state in the economy than they did in the Cárdenas years, mostly because they knew that the government that invited them to Mexico could force them to leave. And their Mexican counterparts found new opportunities in agricultural ventures in Sonora and Sinaloa, where the "green revolution" (subsidized in part by the Ford Foundation, the Agency for International Development, and the World Bank) had been under way since the early 1940s. Nacional Financiera, which directed the state's energies in public enterprises such as railroads, petroleum, and utilities, got funding by selling certificates to Mexican bankers and obtaining credit from the U.S. Export-Import Bank.[15]

These and parallel understandings reinforced economic links but without the complementary political embarrassments that had so often befuddled the Mexican-American relationship. Both governments recognized the reality of intertwined economies; each politely deferred to the other in essentially political expressions of independence. Mexico's nationalistic petroleum policy was illustrative of this governmental role playing and face saving. In August 1946 the U.S. State Department drew up a secret memorandum on the petroleum question. Its essential conclusions were: PEMEX was incapable of developing Mexico's petroleum resources; U.S. oil companies invited to participate in developing Mexican oil should be treated fairly; and the department would not make the mistake of intruding into any arrangements between U.S. oil companies and the Mexican government. The memorandum conveyed the accurate perception that Mexican petroleum development was essentially too political to warrant a vigorous U.S. policy on behalf of American concerns, especially if such a policy might hamper the role of private American capital in other sectors of the Mexican economy. The memorandum recognized Mexico's obvious need for the technical advice and machinery of U.S. petroleum concerns but warned that the Mexican government, for political reasons, must not be pressed on the issue: Mexico must ask for the aid.[16]

As things worked out, the Mexican government developed its petroleum resources as a national *political* enterprise with predictable and inevitable political embarrassments, as a few cynical observers in the State Department were already predicting. But it was clear that the Truman administration—even the often blunt president—had sensed that, for the Mexicans, political gestures were important, and Truman was prepared to accommodate them. In March 1947, a few weeks before proposal for aid to Greece and Turkey, Truman arrived in Mexico City. In the state dinner given in his honor, he denounced international lawlessness but, in words that pleased his Mexican listeners, rejected the unilateral interventionist policies of the past and acknowledged Mexico's commitment to the dignity of the individual. Alemán spoke of the new era in the Mexican–U.S. relationship, where foreign capital and industry were no longer dominant, then promptly declared, "We are bound to live together and prosper together." Truman responded in words that were unintentionally prophetic: "No economic development can take place in either country without producing its effect in the other." Later, in a gesture that endeared him to Mexicans, Truman laid a wreath at the monument to the Niños Heroes, the military cadets who had valiantly defended Mexico City's Chapúltepec heights during the Mexican–American War and plunged to their deaths rather than surrender to the invading Yankees.[17]

The president returned to Washington and formally initiated the cold war with the Truman doctrine. Mexico's official response was ambivalent. As the secretary of PRI declared, "Neither extreme left nor extreme right." This guarded comment implied "we agree with you but cannot, for obvious political reasons, say so." The Communists were promptly expelled from the PRI on the grounds that they were ideologically committed to another party. Mexico's rejection of communism and Alemán's businesslike approach to economic matters were reaffirmed in mid-April 1947 in a high-level banker's conference in Monterrey. The visiting Americans listened politely as a former associate of the U.S. secretary of the treasury spoke about investment opportunities in Mexico, where "the President had already routed communists from power." A week later Alemán (flown on Truman's presidential plane, *The Sacred Cow*) landed at National Airport, where 800,000 Americans, many waving the Mexican flag, cheered as the presidential limousine bore him into the city.[18]

Alemán's was the first state visit of a Mexican president to Washington, and it was rendered doubly significant by the U.S.-Soviet confrontation over postwar European questions and the frantic efforts of U.S. diplomats to woo Latin American countries, especially Mexico, to its anti-Soviet views. Alemán's picture was affixed to lampposts. His triumphant entry into the capital of the nation that had taken half of his country and subjected its governments to innumerable diplomatic indignities was broadcast in 25 languages. He addressed Congress, went on to New York City to get an honorary degree from Columbia, and visited West Point and a Mexican community in Kansas City. When he returned to Mexico City, 750,000 Mexicans thronged the plaza adjacent to the National Palace to greet him. The distinguished Mexican historian, Daniel Cosio Villegas, who had castigated Mexico's postwar leaders for their abandonment of the revolutionary promise of social justice and economic independence, publicly apologized.[19]

His *presidente* had gone into the lair of the nation's enemy and won a spiritual victory. The flush of political pride that swept the country momentarily diverted Mexicans from a less reassuring prospect. Their leader had validated what many feared: he had chosen economic development over social justice.

In reality, however, the choice was unavoidable. It was the consequence of wartime decisions that had generated a vigorous economic growth in both countries. Both the American and Mexican had a higher standard of living in 1950 than they did in 1940. In Mexico a new generation of industrialists, who had emerged to supply the domestic market with manufactures unavailable from the United States during the war, proclaimed "Mexico for the Mexicans," a call for *economic* independence with *Mexican* capital. They pressed the government for ever greater restrictions on imports and less reliance on traditional exports of raw materials and spoke optimistically about Mexico's passage from a "transitional" to a modern economy providing its people with the high-quality consumer goods they deserved. By modernizing its agriculture with irrigation and technology, Mexico would not only be able to produce more foodstuffs but release workers for an expanding industrial labor force.

A modern economy would bring about a modern society went the reasoning. The son of the campesino would migrate to the city and become an unskilled industrial worker. His son would become a skilled worker. His son would become a professional. True, Mexico lacked the economic infrastructure of the United States, but it had achieved a political stability believed impossible a decade before and had exhibited its economic vitality and potential during the war. And with that exaggerated but undeniable sense of national pride Mexico would be able to narrow the gap. There was no desire to create a mirror image of American society or to promote American consumer tastes, only to expand markets for Mexican-made goods among Mexicans of all classes.

But as the Mexican sociologist Pablo González Casanova brilliantly chronicled in the mid-1960s, when the Mexican "economic miracle" was rapidly dissipating in jarring social realities, the "modern Mexico" taking form in the 1940s had yielded a more advanced economy and permitted poor Mexicans to climb a rung or two on the economic ladder but had not broken the social and class barriers that had characterized premodern Mexico.[20] Mexico's postwar leaders were aware of the social consequences of rapid economic change but believed Mexicans of all classes could adapt. They sensed the political risk in favoring industry over agriculture, the agro-export economy over the *ejido,* for such a course meant not abandonment but certainly a lessening of their professed commitments to Mexican campesinos and urban workers.

Yet even in this "dilemma" Mexico's postwar leaders, it has often been argued, might have expended less of the government's energies and resources into economic development and channeled their considerable political might into ameliorating the social and working conditions. A few condemned the "new capitalist order" and called for a socialist Mexico, but this was politically unrealistic and risky. It implied that the postwar leadership had *chosen* a free-enterprise economy and discarded the revolutionary commitment to social justice. In actuality, Alemán's economic program melded the public and private economies in a manner that befuddled American and European observers who accurately described the Mexican economy as "peculiar," a "directed" economy but one lacking a "fixed" plan. As Howard Cline explained in his largely sympathetic assessment of the Mexican economic dilemma in these years, "National economic policies change in accordance with the rise and fall of domestic and international political and economic circumstances. Tugs of war are constantly going on within the country and administration to veer the course one way or another. . . . This is perhaps the only possible course, in view of Mexico's past [but] 'economic democracy' [is] perhaps less perilous than a fixed 'plan' based on needs of the moment and projected infinitely into a yet unpredictable future."[21]

This was not quite accurate. The immediate future was predictable, even if Alemán's generation sensed the inherent dangers in its economic and social legacy for their children. As Mexico industrialized, entrepreneurs and professionals benefitted, increased their purchases of consumer goods, and were rewarded with wage increases. But for industrial and agricultural workers—those who produced the goods demanded by the expanding middle class—*real* wages declined by a third in the 1940s, even as the work force adjusted to more highly productive jobs. The shift to industrial production, understandably, depleted the agricultural labor force (from 65 percent of Mexican laborers in 1940 to 58 percent in 1950), yet these were workers presumably employable in the expanding industrial sector, where their families could reap the benefits of rapidly expanding government social services, particularly in education and health care. Those who were not employable in this capacity joined the generation of agricultural migrants to the United States. Their labor was lost but not the funds they remitted to their families in central Mexico.[22] Through movies and advertising the Mexican government persuaded American tourists (many of them scared away in the 1920s and 1930s) to return to Mexico and spend their dollars.

The cumulative impression was, thus, of a stabler, more prosperous Mexico that had shorn itself of the discord of its revolutionary years. Native capital now went into industry and earned from 8 percent to 20 percent return; indirect foreign, especially American, investment rose dramatically, while continuing to decline in such direct holdings as extractive industries, public utilities, transportation, commerce, and manufacturing. When Ambassador Walter Thurston informed journalist Edgar Snow in the early fifties that total U.S. investments in Mexico had reached $800 million, almost half were in indirect and less "visible" investments. A Mexican president who proudly boasted "Mexico for the Mexicans" was able to distract the traditionally suspicious Mexican from the American penetration of the national economy through purchases of stocks, bonds, or partial ownership of Mexican firms. But the modern investor was now playing by Mexican rules—written and implied. If he did not want to do business the Mexican way, he would not be permitted to do business in Mexico.[23]

In truth, Alemán had reaffirmed Mexican *political* independence but silently acquiesced in the economic domination of the United States. Mexico expanded its role in world trade but sent 75 percent of its exports north. Its exports became more diverse, but in 1950 Mexico remained a nation that increasingly consumed what it did not produce and produced what it did not consume. Confronted with a weakening peso and lessening investor confidence in 1948, Alemán tried to maintain an artificial peso price by borrowing from the International Monetary Fund. That failing, the government devalued the peso, forcing up import prices, which the administration, in turn, had to meet with wage increases. By 1950 Mexican investor confidence returned and exports revived, but the incentives were largely external—tourism, border transactions, and U.S. purchases because of the Korean War.

The Korean War, which began in June 1950, merely accelerated a process already under way after the frenzied purchasing of foreign consumer goods at the end of World War II. Alemán's financial planners quickly established tariffs to protect Mexican manufactures and gave preferential treatment to the importers of machinery and parts for assembly by Mexican workers. Remembering their wartime experience, Mexicans stocked up on high-cost machinery and equipment—mostly from the United States—for the government's ambitious expansionist plans in petroleum, transportation, manufacturing, and agriculture. Greater production and higher quality goods resulted, but Mexico did not break its dependence on foreign technology and capital goods.

chapter 3

THE "MEXICAN MIRACLE"

In March 1950 George Kennan, who had politely questioned the enthusiastic proposals for more ambitious, and costlier, aid programs to Latin America after the war, submitted a now largely forgotten memorandum on U.S. policy in the hemisphere. "Wisdom in Latin American affairs," he advised Secretary of State Dean Acheson, "begins with distrust of the generality." Cursed with an "unhappy and hopeless background" wrought by the dual legacy of natural obstacles and the ferocity of the Spanish conquest and seemingly overwhelmed by a "tremendous helplessness," Latin Americans had survived by "over-compensation." The "splendor and pretense" of their cities compensated for the "wretchedness and squalor" of rural life; the exaggeration of personality was but a "pathetic urge to create the illusion of desperate courage, supreme cleverness, and a limitless virility" in order to mask their lack of "constructive virtues" and failure to create communities. With this ethnocentric comment of the Latin American character, Kennan followed with an exquisitely analytical statement about the dangers of underestimation and overestimation of hemispheric communism. The potential threat was an "urgent, major problem," but Latin "individualism" and "indiscipline" made its Communists unreliable wards of Moscow, which doubtless looked on them with "amusement, contempt, and anxiety." A more immediate danger than broad communist appeal was "clever infiltration of key positions" in governments and the damage to U.S. interests. Kennan's solution was "techniques for coercive measures" that would be sufficiently forceful to persuade Latin America's leaders to get rid of the Communists but not so visibly intrusive as to arouse charges of intervention the Communists could exploit.[1]

The immediate concern about communist influence in the hemisphere involved Guatemala, where a revolutionary government installed in 1944 after the overthrow of the dictator Jorge Ubico had begun to antagonize U.S. business, notably United Fruit Co., with its reformist social program. Guatemala's politics, however, were in the larger scheme of U.S. policy in the hemisphere at mid-century less a direct threat than potentially troublesome. More disturbing to the State Department's long-range planning was Mexico's posture (and place) in the U.S. global anti-Communist strategy. A defiant Guatemalan government could be intimidated or, if necessary, subverted; Mexican leaders, however, were both aware of the nation's vulnerability to U.S. economic power and alert to the *political* risks of visibly knuckling under to American pressures. In April 1951, as Mexican leftists sharpened their attack on Alemán's pro-American policies, a cynical and ironic editorialist wrote, "It is precisely Russia to which we owe our lack of democratic development and growth," which has prevented Mexico from developing a "healthy and advantageous international trade."[2]

The Korean War presented Alemán with numerous problems. From without he was pressed by Americans requesting increased Mexican production of base metals, rubber, and strategic minerals and a prompt resolution of the bracero negotiations, which the two governments had been wrangling over for several years; from within he was pressed by disaffected leftists agitated by reports (quickly denied) that Mexican troops would be dispatched to Korea. The president went to Nuevo Laredo and there met with Texas's governor Allan Shivers and reassured him that Mexico intended to comply with its "international obligations" but expressed concern about the American commitment on the Asian mainland. The political liabilities of repeating the inflationary spiral of World War II were manifest. In August 1950 Alemán sensed an opportunity to enhance the country's international standing by nominating Padillo Nervo as the successor to U.N. Secretary General Trygve Lie. Two leaders of the Mexican Left, Narciso Bassols and Luis Cabrera, declaring that the United Nations was an instrument of war, called for Mexico's withdrawal from that organization. There was revived talk of Soviet espionage in Mexico. The Mexican press published lurid stories on the topic when David Greenglass, an FBI informant in the Rosenberg spy case, referred to the Soviet embassy in Mexico City as a "center in the escape route of Red spies" from the United States. But Alemán's image in the U.S. press did not suffer. As these and other disquieting reports about Mexico's "international obligations" surfaced, he announced that Mexico was committed to the defense of the Western Hemisphere and thus demonstrated, according to an American editorialist, his grasp of geopolitics by reasserting the primacy of "Fortress America."[3]

Within the American government the doubts about Alemán's support for

Washington's Cold War agenda were compared with his anti-Communist policies and the economic accommodations he had already made. In April 1951 a request for Mexican troops was renewed by Thomas Mann (then deputy assistant for inter-American affairs) in a conference with the Mexican foreign minister, Manuel Tello. The need for Mexican soldiers ("well-known for their fighting qualities") in Korea had been brought about by shortages in U.N. forces and the U.S. desire to institute a rotation system as quickly as possible. Mexican troops, unlike those of other Latin American nations, would not require extensive training or large amounts of equipment. Tello praised the U.S. commitment in Korea then abruptly stated that Mexico's support of the U.N. declaration to resist aggression, as was explained to the U.S. ambassador, did not constitute a commitment to furnish troops. Mexican opinion was opposed to such a course. The conversation ended with Mann's oblique reference to the 1952 Mexican presidential campaign ("internal Mexican politics") and a polite recommendation about "preparing and leading Mexican public opinion."[4]

There was, despite Tello's statement, expectation among some U.S. officials that after the election the Mexican government would recognize its international obligations and yield, but the United States "should . . . hammer away at every opportunity on the need for her help *now* rather than at some future date. . . . Our basic economies are completely intertwined. . . . There is no escaping the preponderant role which the United States plays in the whole scheme of living, *but* we must also admit that Mexico is important to the United States."[5] The term "special relationship" in regard to Mexico had not become commonplace in the American press (and was of course too risky for Mexican editorialists), but a State Department secret policy statement in fall 1951 noted Mexico's "special importance" and the U.S. requirement of "stable political and economic conditions" (as before) but now referred to a "sense of common purpose and direction between the two countries." Disputes over air transport, fisheries, agrarian claims, and especially the Chamizal (a narrow strip between El Paso and Ciudad Juárez claimed by Mexico after the Rio Grande shifted course) remained unresolved. Mexicans were distrustful of the United States, and Mexican Communists made the most of this lingering resentment and bitterness. Through economic and especially cultural links, the United States could develop a larger market for American investments and demonstrate "that the moral strength of the United States is as great as its military and financial power."[6]

When in the same year Mexico formally rejected a mutual defense treaty with the United States on the grounds that it would require it to "participate in important missions in defense of the western hemisphere," there was grumbling in Washington that Mexico had, in effect, abandoned a commitment made in Chapúltepec in 1945 and reaffirmed two years later in Rio de Janeiro. The Mexican intent was not abrogation of treaty commitments but Mexico's concern (as its delegates voiced in 1948 in Bogotá) about the military character of hemispheric regional organizations: the ensuing detriment to economic, social, and cultural cooperation in peaceful settlement of disputes; and, more fundamental, the parallel granting of too much political authority to the council of the Organization of American States. As Mexico's economy became more dependent on the United States in the postwar years, its international politics, by necessity of their political image, assumed an independent character. Alemán did not anticipate his successors as third world spokesman, but he did articulate a Mexican view of global conflict. At his direction Mexico's U.N. delegates proposed a resolution requesting the major powers to resolve their disputes by peaceful means, voted against the partition of Palestine, called for more favorable economic treatment for Italy, and announced that Mexico accepted the "complete jurisdiction" of the International Court of Justice. Much of this was, doubtless, political hyperbole in Alemán's campaign to discredit those who charged him with abandoning the revolution, but his stance against the mutual defense agreement with the United States persuaded Mexicans that he understood national self-interest and intended to keep Mexico out of international conflicts that weakened its economy.[7]

Alemán's constituents erred in their belief that he or his chosen successor, Adolfo Ruiz Cortines, would use the state's political resources to redress the social injustices and economic grievances of Mexico's dispossessed. In retrospect, it is easy to see why Washington's cold warriors, looking at Mexico's realistic accommodation of U.S. economic policies, believed that Mexican resistance to the United State's anti-Communist strategies merely represented a lingering bitterness over American political interference in Mexican affairs or yet another manifestation of Mexican uncooperativeness.[8] They believed that, sooner or later, the Mexicans would come round to the American view of the world if only U.S. emissaries would accommodate Mexican pride by tolerating an occasional demurral in the international arena. They presumed, correctly, that Mexico's postwar leaders had chosen to use their inherited political authority to implant a Mexican variation of the Western economic developmental model. But they greatly underestimated the determination and especially the ability of Mexico's *políticos* to shape it to their advantage and to enhance their power.

When Ruiz Cortines took office in December 1952, the principal characteristics of the "Mexican miracle" had taken form. The new president atoned for his predecessor's flashiness and corruption by projecting an image of respectability and dealt with inflationary impulses generated by the Korean War by imposing austerity measures in government. Nevertheless, the policy of import substitution as the impetus to industrialization, advocated by the U.N. Economic Commission for Latin America and generally opposed by the U.S. government, continued. Alemán's economic measures, which had benefitted the business elite of the postwar years, had been made virtually irreversible by Mexico's abrogation of its commerical treaty with the United States in 1951.

The slogan of the Mexican political economy was now "stabilizing development" (*desarrollo estabilizador*).

This and similar policies pleased nationalist business elements, though they
grumbled about the competition from direct foreign investment, especially in
manufacturing. They displeased the Mexican Left. Ruiz Cortines adroitly
compensated by throwing down a challenge to Secretary of State John Foster
Dulles for his harassment of Guatemala's president Jacobo Arbenz. Guatemala's government, Dulles was persuaded, was at the beck and call of international communism. When Dulles carried his campaign into the inter-
American conference at Caracas in March 1954, the Mexicans challenged
him, joining with Argentina and of course Guatemala in denouncing Washington's interventionism. Dulles emerged from Caracas without the vigorous
support he had obviously been seeking from the other hemispheric governments, in part because of Mexico's verbal defiance of Washington's policies.
As the CIA plan ("Operation PBSuccess") to topple Arbenz unfolded, the
State Department commenced an unsubtle psychological campaign in defense
of the U.S. position throughout the hemisphere.

Mexico was singled out for special consideration. There was little belief
within the department that Mexican officials dared risk making a public
statement indicating support for U.S. policy. Ambassador Francis White
sensed, however, that Ruiz Cortines, whose anti-Communist views were well-
known, could be discreetly cultivated but must not be praised. To convey that
Mexico was an ally in this venture would rouse the nation's anti-American
elements, yet to refrain from expressing Washington's noticeable irritation at
Mexico's inhibitions in dealing with Guatemala would, White argued, undermine U.S. credibility in the hemisphere. In Caracas the Mexican position
had rested on the narrow interpretation of nonintervention; Dulles's conten-
tion, on the more elastic version embodied in the Rio de Janeiro treaty. A few
weeks before the Arbenz regime fell in late June 1954, White laid out the
U.S. case against Guatemala in a private session with Mexican Foreign Minister Padillo Nervo, who spoke privately about "moral suasion" but conceded
that if more forceful efforts were necessary to wean the Guatemalans from
their Marxist philsophy, then the Americans should do it. The discussion
ended with a pleasant exchange about the "realistic" way to deal with Communist governments.

The Guatemalan government's fall in a CIA-induced coup prompted another wave of anti-American denunciations in Mexico. Ruiz Cortines and his
coterie said little. Mexico had denied the "legitimacy" of U.S. actions; given
its economic links with the United States, anything more on behalf of Guatemala would have been foolhardy. Communism was less an international than
a domestic problem for Mexico, Ruiz Cortines wrote, and the Mexican people
had generally repudiated the noisy band of Communist leaders in the country.
The U.S. government, in the mistaken belief that Mexico was a "trampolin"
for international communism, had tried to use American economic influence

to "condition the politics of our nation," according to Ruiz Cortines. This view, he explained, implied a lack of confidence in Mexico that the government must overcome by unambiguous statements and actions about national order and international character as Mexicans defined them.[9]

The president had privately acknowledged Mexico's economic dependence but refused, as a matter of national honor and credibility, to render obeisance. Visible accommodations to U.S. pressures were, as Mexicans saw matters, acknowledgment of inferiority. Thus, when President Dwight Eisenhower wrote disapprovingly of the unjustified fears about Mexico's conduct in Caracas and reminded Americans about the new spirit of cooperation between the two governments and the growth of American investments in Mexico, one of Ruiz Cortines's advisors noted, "It would not be convenient [for you] to comment specifically about private investment . . . but [to reaffirm Mexico's] wish for economic cooperation [which] implies solidarity but not uniformity."[10]

A subsumed but disquieting feature of the "Mexican miracle" was the internationalization of Mexican agriculture and the rural labor force that served it. Mexico's political evolution may have diverged sharply from that of the United States, but its agricultural and trade patterns in the North continued to respond to impulses from the vigorous agro-industrial economy in the U.S. Southwest. After the U.S. Civil War, Americans and especially American promoters pushed into the Southwest. Under Porfirio Díaz, the Mexican government tried, fitfully, to respond with colonization schemes for the North. On their collapse, Díaz accepted economic reality and permitted U.S. developers, surveyors, and land concessionaires to penetrate the country. The effect was to orient the economy of the Mexican toward the United States and away from the populous markets of central Mexico. Guadalajara and Mexico City lost out to El Paso, Tucson, Laredo, and Brownsville as commercial entrepôts for the northern Mexican states. Traditional Mexican food crops—corn, beans, squash, and chile—were supplanted by export commodities, and campesinos were moved, sometimes forcibly, to areas where their labor was needed. Revolutionary turmoil and the antiforeign policies of the 1920s and 1930s diminished U.S. land and petroleum holdings and sharply reduced America's presence in mining, but they did not eradicate the regional economic bonds.

There was a human cost in rural development on both sides of the border, its lamentable story hidden in the mythology of the "family farm" in the U.S. experience and the traditional culture of the long-suffering Mexican campesino. The revolutionary agrarian reform of the 1920s and especially the 1930s mitigated some of the harshness of rural life in Mexico. In Texas and New Mexico, however, the migration of Anglo settlers and developers into sparsely settled but resource-scarce areas brought rural farmers, grazers, and ranchers, most of them Americans of Mexican descent, into conflict with the more aggressive—and more numerous—Anglo intruder. Some traced their land titles to grants from the king of Spain. Denied credit or victimized by crooked land surveyors, they lost title to their lands. Many began to steal away for better paying jobs in midwestern industrial towns (joining the black migration from the South). Others tried to organize and were harassed and beaten. Farmers in the Rio Grande Valley soon found a more docile and reliable work force south of the border. In southern California, as Ernesto Galarza has documented, Japanese replaced Chinese as agricultural workers by 1900, but their numbers were dwarfed by a massive Mexican rural work force (from 8,000 to 88,000 by 1920 and 350,000 in 1940). In the 1930s the Mexican Americans often rallied behind the Southern Tenant Farmers Union, which was fighting land evictions under the Agricultural Adjustment Act. The American Federation of Labor had never taken much interest in their cause, and the growers, local chambers of commerce, and Mexican consuls (who did not want to cause problems) joined to break the mutual aid societies and community political organizatons the Mexican Americans had fashioned. A generation of Mexican American farmers in southern California was pushed off the land.[11]

Thus, years before the bracero agreement of World War II gave the practice the official blessing of both governments, southwestern rural interests looked to field hands from Mexico as essential alternatives to the rising cost (and political trouble) of hiring Mexican American workers. Wartime demands for Mexican labor increased the dependence. Mexico found a way to expand the employment of Mexicans and, just as important, to control its troublesome rural population; the United States found a way to fill the enormous manpower shortage of a war economy. But even before war's end, Mexican officials were evincing doubts about a program that had been designed for economic and political purpose but had created political and especially social problems. Braceros recruited from the rain-fed lands of central Mexico knew subsistence farming; in the United States they became hired hands in factories and fields and, despite efforts by both governments to protect their social and political status as legal migrants, in effect, "stateless persons."

In 1943 stories of abusive conditions in Texas prompted the Mexican government to forbid its citizens to work in that state, but the measure was designed principally to placate Mexicans (and other Latin American governments) reading graphic accounts of ill treatment meted out to Mexicans in another country. In the same year occurred the "zoot-suit riots" in Los Angeles, in which Mexican Americans, displaying their cultural defiance in the way they dressed (in extremely cut flashy suits) and behaved, were harassed, beaten, and jailed. There was a difference, of course: the braceros were, technically, guest workers; the zoot-suiters were social provocateurs in their own country. But both had suffered the *social* debility of a Mexican heritage, and when Ezequiel Padilla, Mexico's minister in Washington, denounced the zoot-suiters as subversives in the cause of Mexico and the United States against fascism, some Mexicans were openly critical. Late in the war, the Mexican government dispatched observers into the Southwest who returned with reassuring statements about the well-being of bracero laborers.[12]

After the war, of course, many of these laborers returned home, but their replacements quickly followed and the working conditions for them in the Southwest deteriorated. Even so, the migration of contracted braceros from recruiting stations in central Mexico continued, but, increasingly, *mojados* (laborers who entered the United States illegally, perjoratively referred to as "wetbacks") were joining them. In the late 1940s the preference of growers for "wetbacks" and the eventual yielding of the Mexican government to U.S. pressure to permit recruiting stations in northern Mexico combined to expand an illicit trade in labor. As U.S. growers hired more uncontracted than contracted workers, the Border Patrol of the Immigration and Naturalization Service, understanding the dynamic interplay between southwestern agro-business, immigration practices, and domestic politics, responded by tolerating what immigration laws and bilateral agreements between Mexico and the United States prohibited.

In the diplomatic wrangling after the war, the Mexican government proposed that the employment of undocumented workers in the United States be made "illegal" 40 years before Congress enacted the measure as law in the 1986 immigration reform act. Failure to do so brought a warning about the government's ability to prevent Mexicans from going north to look for work. But, like their American counterparts, the Mexican negotiators recognized the political clout of southwestern agro-businessmen who were determined to have an "open border" so that they might obtain "under conditions favorable to them as many Mexican workers as they needed."[13]

Designed to solve a labor problem, the bracero agreement—renewed in August 1951 after years of diplomatic hassles—was the cause of two others, for both governments. Recruiting stations had been moved north to accommodate U.S. employers, and in the process the numbers of aspirants for jobs with or without contract dramatically increased. In time, the preference of southwestern growers for undocumented workers combined with another, largely unanticipated, outcome of the internationalization of Mexican rural labor: accusations that Mexican recruiters of contract laborers were demanding bribes from hopeful applicants, the deplorable working condition of contracted laborers, and the resulting personal decision of many to flee an abusive employer and join the army of illegal migrants. The social malaise bequeathed by this migration of rootless and, in effect, stateless people who hovered in squalid, mushrooming northern Mexican towns was offensive to Mexican officials. They had, apparently, little choice but to accept it as an inevitable byproduct of the Anglo's insatiable demand for Mexican labor.

But the deplorable conditions in squatter communities on the U.S. side of the border jolted a United States conditioned to postwar prosperity. In March 1951 the *New York Times* described the coexistence of "two Americas" in the

Southwest: one prosperous, the other wretched. The annual "invasion" of a million "border jumpers" from cardboard shanty towns into a region where the Mexican American population had not yet caught up in living standards with Anglos had diminished the quality of social services and, further, was "lowering culture," as the "illegals" were forming a "vast, unassimilable block." The Border Patrol, caught between a federal government anxious to respond to criticism from organized labor and the needs of southwestern agro-business, was understandably ambivalent about what should be done. In this regard, Truman perceived that the bracero agreement would not do away with the social and economic injustices suffered by Mexican farm labor in the United States. Organized labor in both countries spoke disapprovingly of working conditions on southwestern farms. Sen. Dennis Chávez of New Mexico, who had trumpeted the cause of English-language instruction in New Mexico schools in the 1930s, warned of the debasement of rural labor, and a Jalisco labor organizer wrote Alemán in an appeal for his support of a Union of Workers to protect Mexican farm laborers in the United States. Mexican workers were divided on this issue. The Federal District branch of the Mexican Confederation of Labor indicted the braceros for abandoning their families and Mexican factories in search of the gringo's dollar. Organized labor in both countries sustained political pressure to ameliorate the working and living conditions of Mexican field hands in the Southwest.[14]

By this time, of course, the number of Mexicans illegally entering the country had strained the resources of the Border Patrol, whose function it was to apprehend them, and the courts, whose purpose it was to adjudicate their cases. Roy Rubottom, then occupying the Mexico desk in the State Department, had succinctly analyzed the U.S. dilemma in a 1950 memorandum: "Legalization of wetbacks is the most practical method of extricating ourselves from this situation. This approach will make no difference in the Lower Valley [of Texas] . . . since the wetbacks are already there by the thousands and are still flooding in. . . . The courts are so crowded that deportation cases are stacking up. INS has insufficient personnel to carry out its program of rounding up wetbacks for voluntary deportation. The situation is bad and could hardly be worse."[15] Almost three years after this morose assessment and two years after the 1951 agreement designed to correct it, the situation was, indeed, worse. Destitute Mexican farmers, driven from the land by the combination of five years of drought and the lessening demand for agricultural exports, had invaded Mexican towns looking for work. Unable to find it because of cutbacks in Mexico's public sector, they had joined countrymen headed north, where even the lowly wages paid to undocumented workers exceeded the $1 a day average wage in Mexico.[16]

As Eisenhower planned for his meeting with Ruiz Cortines on the Texas border in the fall of 1953 to dedicate the Falcon Dam, the Justice Department had resorted to calling on the army and national guard to repel the "wetback invasion." The "undesirable traffic," Assistant Secretary of State John Cabot explained to Ambassador White, had created social problems in southern California, where undocumented workers had become violent. The Mexican government persisted with requests that "we crack down on the farmers" who hire them, wrote Cabot, but this was "not possible for political reasons." There had to be another method. White was aghast. He had labored hard to make the Falcon Dam meeting a success, drawing vivid contrasts between the official cooperation on the U.S.–Mexican border and the iron curtain of Europe. "We won't be able to make capital out of that if we have bayonets and muskets on the border."[17]

The meeting at Falcon Dam was outwardly cordial, but the Justice Department continued to pursue the military option. Shortly after the expiration of the bracero agreement in December 1953, Attorney General Herbert Brownell estimated the number of "illegals" in the country at 4 million (half of them employed in industry) and attributed to their presence a "grave social problem, involving murder, prostitution, robbery, and narcotics." The Mexican government was caught off guard by the severity of Brownell's words, though no longer befuddled by a U.S. government that blamed it for permitting its people to migrate north looking for work but did not indict its own people for employing them. In June, using as excuse the illegal entry of "subversives," the U.S. goverment commenced "Operation Wetback," expelling a million by the end of the year and 250,000 in 1955. As U.S. farm union organizers had argued, wages and working conditions for Mexican American rural laborers, especially in the Rio Grande Valley of Texas, improved dramatically. Those expelled suffered humiliation, abuse, and disruption of family. Men forced to leave abandoned their wives and children. The psychological effect of the massive deportation of fellow Mexicans, however, wrote two chroniclers of the Chicano experience, "reinforced traditional mistrust of the United States government among Mexican Americans and . . . increased feelings of alienation from Anglo society."[18]

As a solution to the problem of illegal entry of Mexican labor, "Operation Wetback" was a failure, and both governments knew it. The Mexican American rural laborer benefitted momentarily, it is true, but in the course of the decade he continued to move into the cities, and the Mexican came back to take his place on southwestern farms. An international migration begat a domestic migration. The social dynamic created by this movement of peoples of a common heritage but of different nations was of uncertain outcome, but neither government was prepared to live with the kind of practices necessary to enforce the immigration law along a 2,000-mile border that divided two nations but not their economies. Reports telling of the use of dogs by the Border Patrol to round up undocumented workers in Texas aroused the press and embarrassed the Justice Department when Mexican officials made denigrating comparisons with Soviet-bloc countries.[19]

What could be more precisely calculated were the benefits for two economies that were rapidly becoming interdependent. Mexico's "economic miracle" was predicated on export agriculture and industrialization, which required, as both Mexican and American observers believed, technology and capital investment. U.S. direct investments in Mexico (principally in manufacturing, mining, transportation, and utilities), which under the benevolent Alemán had risen to $728 million in 1952, rose dramatically to $1.2 billion by 1957. Alert to leftist criticism of its inducements to foreign capitalists, the Ruiz Cortines government publicized the number of firms that had been "Mexicanized," but even in these the reach of the American investor was strong.[20]

Where the two governments differed, sometimes sharply, was how best to accomplish modernization, and for what social purpose. Encouraging the growth of a corporate culture and a consumer society at home, Eisenhower and his advisors enthusiastically lauded a vigorous private sector for Latin America, especially Mexico, and saw correctly that the principal beneficiaries of the "economic miracle" next door would be the middle class. For the United States, the benefits were economic and political—an expanding economy next door that supplied labor for U.S. agro-business and a growing middle class to purchase U.S. products, emulate American culture, and, in time, "Americanize" Mexican politics and politicians.

Having gone to so much trouble to create and maintain the political system, of course, Mexican leaders were loath to do anything that might undermine their power. In the United States political fortune depends less on ideology than economic conditions; in Mexico it depends on the survival instincts of those in power. Theirs was a dual task: to "stabilize development," which required foreign (principally American) investment, hard currency, and a friendly private sector; and to stabilize politics, which called for credibility in the often stormy political climate.

In brief, then, the government's task was to persuade the self-professed heirs of the revolution, most notably Cárdenas, and their followers that the revolutionary commitment to social justice remained strong, and, simultaneously, to convince those who were financing and sustaining the "economic miracle" that the government was an ally. Satisfying both was, of course, impossible. The impressive gains in export agriculture, especially in the Northwest, had brought opportunity to owners of large farms, but the living standards of campesinos had not appreciably improved. Migrants from impoverished regions squatted illegally on productive farmlands and were driven off by guards or the military. Some joined the migration north to the border, others became internal migrants, working on plantations, or headed for the city, where they joined the armies of *los olvidados* ("the forgotten ones"). Inequities in the social structure of 1950 remained in 1960. Mexico's upper 10 percent absorbed 10 percent of the nation's wealth in 1950 and retained that share in 1960. The middle class grew and, unquestionably, fared better in

1960 than in 1950 despite the sharp rise in living costs; the lower classes had also grown but lived worse. Rural Mexico was poorer by virtually every measure.[21]

Confronted with this unsettling prospect, the Mexican government in the mid-1950s chose economic development over equity on the judgment that greater employment and more consumer goods were preferable to social justice for the lower classes. This strategy made economic sense to the U.S. government, but U.S. officials demurred over the means by which the Mexicans carried it out. Unlike Eisenhower's America, Mexico was too dependent on external forces for its economic vitality. In the economic downturn after the Korean War, Mexican exports (particularly cotton, the unintended victim of U.S. agricultural policy) declined, from $807 million in 1956 to $600 million in 1958. Determined to continue with its industrialization program, the government had to rely on more than export earnings—tourism, remittances from Mexican farm workers in the United States, foreign investments (which escalated by 60 percent between 1952 and 1958), and loans from international lending agencies, particularly the Export-Import Bank.

In all of these the U.S. economic presence was crucial, and American lecturing about Mexican "statism" unrelenting. Most of the external funding for development went into large business, precipitating complaints from 8,000 small and medium-size concerns (organized into a national chamber), which competed with them and called for restrictions on foreign investments. The government listened and decided to accommodate both by continuing to secure external financing and, at the same time, to subsidize the private sector in low-cost goods and services from state enterprises. American officials regularly complained that such a mix of politics and economics would be ruinous; their Mexican counterparts generally responded that such a course— however irrational in U.S. economic policy—made sense for Mexico.[22]

"Officially cordial, privately disagreeable" would be an apt description of the diplomatic relationship in the 1950s. American officials publicly lauded Mexico's newfound political stability and economic progress and, in occasionally hortatory but generally unpersuasive private commentaries, warned Mexican leaders about the political ills that followed statist policies. The word *técnicos* appeared in the political lexicon to characterize a new type of Mexican official less given to assailing Yankee imperialists than to encouraging Yankee investors. Still, the latent political resentments against previous U.S. interference remained and, when combined with the concerns of the *técnicos* about Mexico's economic dependence, prompted even the pro-American Ruiz Cortines to restrict foreigners in "positions of influence" in businesses or industries not covered by Mexican labor laws. There followed predictable and sometimes justifiable complaints about contradictory signals—one ministry of the Mexican government (Commerce) would encourage the investor while another (Interior) would simultaneously harass him with silly requirements over the "Mexicanization" of his managerial force.[23]

In words that Mexicans had grown accustomed to hearing, U.S. officials spoke of "unfortunate repercussions" in the wake of such regulations and attributed them to the "inordinate nationalism . . . innate in the Mexican national character." But with the collapse of the 1943 trade agreement, they could do little more than protest Mexican policies, warning the Mexicans, as did Ambassador White, about the "primary objectives of the Communists in all of Latin America to break down . . . economies . . . by . . . having as many enterprises as possible taken over and run by the government because they know they will not be as effectively administered as in private hands" or persisting in their conviction that Mexico's need for Export-Import Bank loans ultimately dictated "improvement in her policies."[24]

Accommodating the U.S. economic presence, the Mexicans nonetheless refused to follow Washington's preachments about the role of government in the economy and at the same time resisted demands from the Left for a renewal of Cárdenas policies. The government expanded opportunities for Mexican industrialists and manufacturers in the growing domestic market and continued statist economic policies, which pleased the nationalists but displeased U.S. officials. And when analysts in the U.S. embassy heartened to rumors of a Mexican military that was "fed up" or the prospects for a political challenger from the conservative wing of the PRI party, the government promptly squelched the pretenders and simultaneously reassured its American critics with new economic pronouncements! It was yet another example of the Mexican ability to stifle pro-American party members yet adjust to U.S. pressures. In late 1955, for example, Ruiz Cortines presented a balanced budget for the following year and declared, in words that obviously pleased his American listeners, "the economic policy of the balanced budget will continue inflexibly."[25]

Given the political realities that prevailed in Mexico, especially the growing unrest in labor and in the countryside and the accompanying economic demands on the government, Ruiz Cortines's 1955 pronouncement was a doomed pledge. But it was issued more to reassure the U.S. government and investor that Mexico had a bright economic future and, at the same time, to persuade Washington that Mexico had developed a political economy that must be accommodated. Mexico's revolutionary titans of the past had confronted twin challenges to their rule: one from within, the other from the United States. By 1958, as the nation entered yet another *sexenio* (six-year presidency) with Adolfo López Mateos, Mexico's leaders had been able to fend off the external political threat by patient and expedient policies. But the price of yielding to U.S. economic intrusion was a revival of the internal challenge, largely but not exclusively from the Left, from those who said that Mexico's postwar leaders had abandoned the revolutionary commitment for an American dollar.

In international affairs, especially in the Western Hemisphere, Mexico had severed military but not economic ties with the United States, declared its neutrality in the cold war, and, during the 1954 Guatemalan crisis, reaffirmed its commitment to nonintervention. But in rejecting Washington's cold war agenda, Mexico's leaders had neither returned to the confrontationist policies of the Calles or Cárdenas years nor sought an active role in the nonaligned movement taking shape in the third world. Mexico belonged to the United Nations and the Organization of American States and had signed the Inter-American Treaty of Reciprocal Assistance, which Secretary of State Dulles had cleverly exploited to undermine a leftist government in neighboring Guatemala. Mexico was a member of the international community over which Washington exercised dominion. But Mexico did not always conform to American dictates, and when it did follow the U.S. lead in world affairs, its justification generally depended on the domestic political situation. In any case, the Eisenhower administration acquiesced in Mexico's independent and occasionally defiant foreign policy.

Such unaccustomed deference meant little to Mexico's *políticos* as they prepared for the inauguration of López in 1958. They had deeper concerns than the voiced displeasures of the Eisenhower administration over Mexico's demurral to the Guatemalan operation or Washington's grumbling about Mexico's economic policy. A demographic revolution had profoundly changed the social and economic character of the nation. Mexico's population had almost doubled (from 16 to 32 million) since Cárdenas had become president in 1934; it had industrialized; its cities, especially the federal district, had mushroomed; and a middle class emerged. But as leftist critics recalled, the price had been the loss of autonomous economic development and the penetration of U.S. companies and culture, which strengthened Mexico's dependence and weakened its sense of national identity. Mexico's new president was youthful, energetic, and inspiring to a population weary of revolutionary platitudes. Those who had come of age since the harsh 1930s, when ordinary campesinos lived in a subsistence economy, had no memory of the social despair of the Depression, but they sensed the revolution had not fulfilled its promise. The "economic miracle" had produced a richer, more abundant, and certainly more industrialized Mexico, but it had not created a more equitable society. As secretary of labor in Ruiz Cortines's cabinet, López had expressed sympathy for Mexico's laborers, particularly its industrial workers, and had declared in his campaign that as Mexico's next president he was determined to shift the revolution to the left. Worker's rights must be respected, he told Mexicans, and in the countryside, where agrarian reform had slowed under a relentless program to expand the agro-export economy, López pledged that landless campesinos were entitled to social justice.

These were compelling promises. Cárdenas, now recognized as the legitimate voice of the revolutionary tradition, supported López, as did Mexico's youth, who were persuaded that the country's impressive economic productivity, if directed toward the resolution of social problems, would fulfill the promise of a more equitable and just society. Within a decade their dreams had vanished, for theirs was a nation whose leaders had chosen development over equity.[26]

The political legacy of this choice did not register on the hemispheric community until 1968, when middle-class Mexicans denounced the government's firing on and killing hundreds of otherwise peaceful marching protestors in northern Mexico City. But the social consequences had appeared much earlier and were attributable to presidential decisions. Ruiz Cortines had expanded the state's presence in the economy by creating 29 administrative entities but had simultaneously reassured business by offering incentives to the private sector. The result was that more than 50 percent of public expenditures in his *sexenio* were allocated to industrial development and the private sector.

Business's favorable response was immediate, but Ruiz's reluctance to antagonize the private sector by using government authority to intrude in labor–management disputes roused Mexican labor, which had been suffering a decrease in real wages since 1939. The protest brought an upward trend in social expenditures, but it was clear that the revolutionary heirs had made a fundamental choice in economic policy. Mexico's future, they had determined, depended primarily on the private sector and secondarily on the government's willingness to address persistent social injustices. Cynical observers now reminded Mexicans that in 1910, on the eve of the revolution, there were "two Mexicos." A half-century later, the two Mexicos remained.

chapter 4

TIES THAT BIND

In Díaz's Mexico campesinos and laborers bore the economic and social burden of industrialization; in the "economic miracle" of the 1950s the low wages of industrial workers and the continuing poverty of rural people proved that, despite more than three decades of social legislation and agrarian reform, they had yet to reap the benefits. Mexico's industrialists sensed the dilemma that Adolfo López Mateos confronted, but they had a dilemma of their own—their economic position was now jeopardized by the rising amount of imported consumer goods that competed with domestic products. They needed technology, capital, and a protected market; in brief, they could ill afford to lose their share of government support to social programs that required sustained financing and, inevitably, a fundamental alteration in the country's tax structure.

Earlier, Mexico's business moguls might have mobilized under a rightist political umbrella, but López instinctively understood that they did not have this option. His cabinet was dominated by *técnicos* and centrists. Leftists, who decried the American economic penetration and the gulf between rural and urban Mexico, anticipated that his *sexenio* meant no fundamental reversal of the economic policies of his predecessor. López addressed the Left in his 1958 inaugural, in a manner reminiscent of Díaz's stricture of "bread or the stick," by promising bold new educational measures but adding the caveat, "Liberty is fruitful only when it is accompanied by order. Liberty without order is anarchy, and order without liberty is dictatorship." Secretary of State Dulles, heading the U.S. delegation at the inauguration, was doubtless pleased.

López commenced his *sexenio* by reasserting executive power. When labor strikes precipitated by rising prices spread to the national rail system, in which a Communist headed a militant union, López broke the strike with troops, then began cracking down on other Mexican Communists, among them David Siqueiros, the famous muralist and putative Soviet agent, who was thrown in jail. Having applied the rod to remind labor where political authority in Mexico resides, López followed with a broad program that incorporated labor into Mexico's social security program, allocated education the biggest share of the national budget, commenced a land-distribution program that rivaled Cárdenas's in the 1930s, built low-income housing in Mexico City's Federal District, and created a government entity to stabilize the market of basic foodstuffs, presumably assuring that the poor's nutritional needs would be met. In a mining law of 1960 the government extended concessions to national capital. It began purchasing foreign-controlled electric power companies (in part with loans from Prudential Life Insurance Co. and other U.S. lending institutions), took over the Mexican motion picture industry, announced—to the consternation of foreign petroleum concerns—plans for state control of 18 of 21 future petrochemical plants, and, to expand car ownership, gave preferential tariff concessions to four-cylinder automobiles. At the same time, López told foreign auto manufacturers they must assemble their cars in Mexico or leave the country.[1]

As he had promised, López shifted left, but in Cuba another revolutionary leader, Fidel Castro, was already calling for a more drastic solution to the social injustices that economic modernization had failed to resolve—a fundamental restructuring of the Cuban economy, which, Castro soon demonstrated, required a remolding of Cuban political culture. The Cuban revolution strongly appealed to Mexican leftists. Castro had trained in Mexico following his release from imprisonment on the Isle of Youth in 1955.

The deteriorating U.S.–Cuban relationship culminated in a formal diplomatic break in January 1961, the April 1961 Bay of Pigs invasion, the expulsion of the Cuban government from the OAS, and the Missile Crisis of October 1962. Each incident fueled the revival of debate over Mexico's own revolution, its legacy, and its future.

Throughout this tense period of the early 1960s, the Mexican government maintained a formal, if strained, diplomatic link with the Cubans, resisted the increasing pressure from Washington on hemispheric governments to sever their ties with Cuba, and frustrated the efforts of pro-Castro Mexicans who denounced López's policy. Initially, at least, the decision to risk Washington's wrath had little to do with any presumed Mexican identification with a fellow Latin revolutionary. Rather, Mexico's position on the Cuban issue was yet another validation of the stand taken in Caracas five years before, when the Mexican delegate, citing the principles of self-determination and nonintervention, joined those who abstained on the critical vote on communism in the Americas. Yet in refusing to sanction Washington's pressures on Castro, López knew the Americans would take economic retaliation—as, indeed, a

U.S. senator admitted was the case during a debate over economic policy in the mid-1960s—but López also knew that if he acquiesced and broke with Castro, there would be political hell to pay in his country.[2]

Had the Caribbean crisis not escalated into a hemispheric battle, López might have been able to maintain Mexican neutrality, but he was increasingly pressed by external and internal forces on the Cuban issue. The Eisenhower and especially the Kennedy administration insisted on Latin American compatibility with U.S. policy toward Cuba as an important criterion in assessing economic aid requests. But a more troubling problem for López came from within the country. There was little fear that the Mexican revolution, inspired by Castro's example, would turn dramatically to the left. As the hemispheric political situation worsened, Mexican businessmen grew fretful over the impact on investor confidence in Mexico. With the Soviet link (first economic, then military) Cuba had made Mexican neutrality a risky matter. Mexican investors were especially chagrined when López publicly reaffirmed Mexico's commitment to self-determination and nonintervention. They suggested that Mexico should try to mediate between Washington and Havana, reminding López that in early 1960, when the Mexican government came perilously close to another peso devaluation, the U.S. government and the International Monetary Fund had come to its rescue.

But López was not yet persuaded. Indeed, the government appeared to move more aggressively against foreign companies. It bought the last of Mexico's privately owned electric utilities, expanded its control of national resources, and proudly announced the policy of "Mexicanization" of foreign-owned companies, a process requiring majority ownership by Mexican nationals. The impression conveyed by such measures was that López was not going to back down, and if he had to choose between placating the Right or the Left, he would choose the latter. Sometime later, when hemispheric ministers of foreign affairs gathered in San José, Costa Rica, the Mexicans listened politely as American delegates spoke of U.S. support for the newly created Inter-American Development Bank and the dangers of communism. Mexico's fellow Latins responded with pleas for economic development assistance. When the United States' delegation pressed for sanctions against Cuba for exporting revolution, Mexico refused to go along. (Mexico reluctantly approved a resolution declaring that the inter-American system was "incompatible" with Communism.) There followed a noticeable drop in investor confidence, a run on the dollar, and a capital flight to U.S. and European banks.[3]

This was persuasive evidence to some that López had meant what he had said about a political course as far left as he could get under the Mexican constitution. Private-sector spokesmen demanded a clarification of his economic policies. López began a subtle shift back toward the center. At San José Mexico had opposed sanctions against Cuba, but it had also rebuked the Cubans for inviting the Soviets into hemispheric affairs. The government was indeed strengthening its economic grip, he told investors, but only in those areas where the private sector could not efficiently operate. There was no conflict between government and the private sector; on the contrary, López declared, they complemented one another.

These were not totally reassuring words to either Left or Right, of course, but López was demonstrating that instinctive ability of modern Mexican leaders to mitigate political tensions without resolving them. As the Alliance for Progress and the U.S. war against Castro got under way in 1961, he made more conciliatory gestures. Dutifully, he condemned the Bay of Pigs invasion, which pleased the Left, then followed with gestures at Punta del Este I, where hemispheric foreign ministers set down alliance goals, and especially at Punta del Este II, when the Cuban government was expelled from the OAS, which placated the Left, the Right, and the United States. At both conferences Mexico reaffirmed its commitment to self-determination and nonintervention. At the second, Mexico announced that Marxism-Leninism and OAS membership were incompatible, yet the Mexican representative could not accept a proposal to expel a Marxist-Leninist government from the OAS nor approve economic sanctions against Cuba because there was no firm legal basis for doing so within that organization. Subsequently Mexican foreign minister Manuel Tello appeared with the Mexican ambassador to the OAS and a prominent Mexican senator on U.S. television to explain government policy. The senator was, doubtless, the most effective when he said, "Mexico is not communist . . . [and] could never be a communist country."[4]

His reassurance had less to do with common antipathies to communism than a political reality no Mexican leader could publicly acknowledge (then or now)—the intertwining of two economies. Even in 1950, as Mexican spokesmen took a solitary position in defiance of U.S. policy in the hemisphere or railed against "economic imperialism," they had quietly tightened the bonds of two economies—in their reliance on U.S. investments, in their agricultural policies, and in their dispatch of Mexican laborers northward. In his 1947 visit to the United States, Miguel Alemán had spoken eloquently about this process: "It is the responsibility of all of us to add to the Good Neighbor policy a Good Neighbor economy. Whatever Mexico and the United States achieve will serve Mexico and the United States, but it will also serve all of America, for the border of our republics is a connecting point, a touchstone for guiding the future manifestations of hemispheric contacts."[5]

Mexico in 1960 was a more diversified, more advanced, but an undeniably dependent economy. A more cynical, but doubtless more accurate, interpretation of the consequences of this bond in 1960 was penned by Oscar Lewis, the noted anthropologist, whose pathbreaking study of urban poverty in Mexico City, *The Children of Sánchez,* appeared the following year. Commenting on the revolutionary mythology, Lewis succinctly catalogued its social failure: "Over 60 per cent of the population are still ill fed, ill clothed and ill housed, over 40 per cent are illiterate, and some 45 per cent of the nation's children are not being schooled. The national wealth has greatly increased since 1940, but the disparity between rich and poor is even more striking than before, despite some rise in the general standard of living."[6]

With such indictments, which knowledgeable observers validated, the Kennedy administration confronted in Mexico compelling evidence of the need for a massive aid program under the auspices of the Alliance for Progress. The Mexicans wanted development aid and were of course flattered by the attentiveness of the new American president, who pointed to Mexico as a model for the rest of Latin America. But they had no intention of spending the major portion of alliance monies on social programs. To have done so would have acknowledged the validity of what their critics had been saying, and, besides, it was politically beneficial for the government to announce a new housing or educational program or give some worthless land to a few Indian families. Rather, as result of Punta del Este I, Mexico's political and private-sector elites momentarily ceased their public sniping at one another and joined forces in the pursuit of the dollar. U.S. investors learned again of Mexico's tough stand against communism at home, and the Mexican tourist bureau stepped up its promotion of the nation as a vacationer's paradise. The campaign was effective and, when coupled with the significant remissions of Mexican workers in the United States, enabled the Mexicans to boast that Mexico had achieved the "peaceful revolution" of which Kennedy spoke.

Privately, of course, this assessment was less optimistic. In March 1962 López received an analysis of Mexico's economic condition that called for a three-year development plan under the general guidelines of the Alliance for Progress. The plan was not publicized, as it proposed a retrenchment of state involvement in the industrial and manufacturing sector, a strengthening of economic ties with the United States, further efforts to meet social needs through public works projects, and, most critically, much greater spending to increase productivity in agriculture. A few months later, as he prepared to host President and Mrs. Kennedy for a much-publicized Mexican visit, López unveiled yet another plan for the industrial and manufacturing sector: 500 new enterprises in a five-year period. With greater agricultural productivity and growth in industry and manufacturing, Mexico would be able to feed itself and create a larger market for Mexican products, at home and abroad.[7]

Curiously, few of the histories of Mexican–U.S. relations acknowledge that Mexico was a major recipient of Alliance for Progress funding or, indeed, supported the program.[8] The government's major concerns with the United States, it appeared, were on the frontier, especially in the long-standing dispute over the Chamizal strip (an area of Mexican soil between El Paso and Ciudad Juárez) and over Mexico's complaints about the salinity of Colorado River water passing into Mexico. When President and Mrs. Kennedy arrived in Mexico City in summer 1962, Kennedy agreed that the Chamizal strip, diverted to the U.S. side when the Rio Grande changed its course in 1864, would be restored to Mexico. The Colorado salinity problem, they decided, required further investigation.[9]

Where Cuba was concerned, most observers anticipated fundamental disagreement, if not a rancorous private exchange. But in their joint communiqué, Kennedy and López, as if following a script, expressed their common determination "to oppose totalitarian institutions and activities which are incompatible with the democratic principles they hold" and "to respect and maintain the principles of nonintervention . . . and of self-determination of peoples."[10] There was no specific mention of Cuba, though the Mexican ambassador to that county returned to Mexico City before Kennedy arrived, fueling speculation that Mexico's position on the Cuban question was being reconsidered. Indeed, Kennedy was effusive in his affirmation that the goals of the Alliance for Progress and the Mexican revolution—"social justice and economic progress within the framework of individual freedom and political liberty"—were the same. Despite its economic success and, presumably, the greater need elsewhere in Latin America, Mexico was a major recipient of Alliance funding in 1961 and 1962 (ranking third, after Brazil and Chile, in 1961), receiving $106 million in developmental assistance in the first year of the alliance and $162 million in the second.[11]

The Mexican reception to the Kennedys was one of the most enthusiastic ever accorded to a U.S. president anywhere in Latin America and, in what was particularly embarrassing for the Mexican leader, greater than that accorded any Mexican president before. López was publicly gracious and polite but furious at his counselors who had assured him that his leftist course would assure his popularity with Mexicans. They shouted vivas for Kennedy but not for him. When the President and Mrs. Kennedy laid a wreath at the Monument to the Revolution, several in the crowd began calling out, "*Muerte a los ateos*" (Death to the atheists), which others quickly changed to "*Muerte a López Mateos.*" U.S. intelligence agents made much of this and other embarrassments for the Mexican leader in their evaluation of the Kennedy visit. The most obvious conclusion was that López's shift to the "left within the constitution" had antagonized the emerging middle class.[12]

Such was the American perception of López's political error. As is often the case when U.S. officials assess Mexican politics, the perception served as yet another diversion from a disturbing reality: Mexico's economic policy had stimulated development but had not yielded equity, yet Kennedy had committed the United States to the Mexican developmental model. Two governments with sharply different hemispheric policies, differing political structures, and differing social priorities had created an economic community in North America. Despite the verbal battles over Guatemala and Cuba and the vexing disputes over Mexico's economic statism in the postwar era, the economic ties remained. The character of the economic relationship had changed, but the relationship had not noticeably weakened. As Kennedy said of the relationship, "Geography has made us neighbors, tradition has made us friends, economics has made us partners." The vaunted "shift to the left" had yielded Mexican defiance in the hemispheric crisis but had not severed the economic partnership.

With the Missile Crisis of October 1962, López again found himself in a predicament. Given the seriousness of the crisis and Kennedy's condemnation of Soviet action as a hemispheric threat, López could ill afford to risk U.S. economic retaliation by condemning the U.S. decision to quarantine Cuba. As in other crises, however, the Mexicans skillfully separated themselves from the American camp in the ensuing diplomatic confrontation in the United Nations and OAS. Mexico voted affirmatively in the OAS on the motion to demand that the Soviets remove the missiles but qualified its support with the condition that Washington must not invade the island. When in the following year the Venezuelan government condemned Castro for fomenting guerrilla war in Venezuela and joined Washington in calling on hemispheric governments to impose economic sanctions on and sever diplomatic relations with Cuba, Mexico declared that it would not cooperate. Mexico lost out in the debate when the OAS council called on those member states that still had diplomatic ties with Cuba—Uruguay, Chile, Bolivia, and Mexico—to sever the relationship.

All countries save Mexico agreed. Yet the Mexican government did not noticeably suffer, politically or economically, by this diplomatic contretemps. The U.S. ambassador in Mexico City promptly announced that Mexico's decision was a matter of principle—the defense of nonintervention. Mexico was a friend not a satellite, he declared. In the aftermath, Mexican officials made sure the Cubans did not misinterpret this decision. They closely monitored Havana–Mexico City traffic by blacklisting Mexican visitors to Cuba and seizing any Cuban books, magazines, or other material of a political nature that these visitors tried to bring back into Mexico. Such actions were yet another way of reminding U.S. leaders and especially American investors that Mexico was safe from any Cuban influence.[13]

Subsequently both Kennedy and López became world travelers—Kennedy to Europe, López to the nonaligned Asian countries of India and Indonesia and then to France, Poland, and Yugoslavia. The move was a signal that Mexico was at last determined to break the economic grip of its northern neighbor by diversifying its trade. The gains were modest but significant. Seventy-five percent of Mexico's foreign trade in 1955 had been with the United States; when López passed the presidential sash to Gustavo Díaz Ordaz in 1964, it was less than 70 percent. In those years Mexico had tried to broaden its economic ties with other Latin American countries, then organizing a weak economic confederation, but the competitive character of their economies did not make for a robust economic relationship.[14]

Of far greater economic—and, ultimately, political—significance for Mexico was the rapid economic and demographic transformation of the 2,000-mile frontier to the north and the related matter of growing problems in rural

Mexico. One had to do with the internationalization of North American agriculture and the migration of agricultural workers, mostly from central Mexico, into the U.S. Southwest. This was a movement of labor that dramatically affected the supply of rural workers in Mexico and the union struggle for improved working conditions on farms in the United States.

The second issue dealt with the militance of rural farm workers (campesinos) who were squatting on private land. The economic embargo imposed by Washington on Cuba, which Mexico had officially denounced, nonetheless served Mexican agro-business. Two years before Castro took power, 60 percent of Mexico's agricultural exports (principally cotton, vegetables, and sugar) were destined for the foreign market. Two percent of Mexican farms, employing 3 million rural laborers, accounted for 70 percent of this agricultural bounty. The end of U.S.–Cuban trade enabled Mexican growers, many of them financed by American brokers, to increase production. This meant, of course, expanding the amount of acreage in production, which required a larger pool of farm workers. And it also signalled a confrontation, especially in the agricultural regions of northwestern Mexico, between farmers and landless campesinos, both of whom looked to Mexico City for support.

In Baja California and Sonora, farm workers and campesinos organized the Independent Peasant Confederation. Led by Communists, they launched strikes and began illegal occupation of land. If López's words about "getting as far left as possible under the constitution" meant anything, they were persuaded; they believed that the government would sustain their cause. Indeed, the Mexican president invigorated the *ejido* program (López and Díaz Ordaz boasted they had collectively granted 37 million acres to 500,000 campesinos), but his police and soldiers, assisted by the U.S. FBI, waged a repressive campaign against the confederation. Such confrontations worsened the lot of rural Mexicans and drove more of them into the bracero labor pool and, if unable to contract for legal entry into the United States, into the growing army of undocumented workers.

By the time of Kennedy's visit in summer 1962, the situation in the countryside had become critical. The Mexicans correctly anticipated that the bracero program, based on U.S. Public Law 78 of 1951, would shortly expire. At first glance, the program appeared to be mutually beneficial. Southwest growers who were able to show that domestic workers were unavailable, with the approval of the Department of Labor, contracted for braceros at regional offices in Mexico, thus employing Mexican workers and ensuring lower prices for American food consumers. The problem was the interpretation of the program's guidelines and requirements in two different political systems. By the end of the 1950s often rancorous disputes were breaking out in the United States among a variety of pressure groups, ranging from organized labor to growers and consumer organizations. Within the Eisenhower and Kennedy administrations, the issue precipitated ever-deepening conflict between the Departments of Agriculture and Labor—the former in informal political alliance with southwestern growers and state governments, the latter, increasingly, a sympathetic voice for unions and consumer groups.[15]

The bracero program and what to do about it became a political litmus test on both sides of the border. The issue impinged on U.S. immigration law, the farm union movement, mechanization in agriculture, and Mexican–U.S. negotiations. Created by two governments, the program had become by the end of the 1950s the most visible element in a more complex, and thus more lasting, economic pattern. With the legal migration of Mexican farm workers in the 1950s had grown a migration of rootless Mexicans who entered the United States undocumented. "Operation Wetback" of 1954 significantly reduced the number of illegal entries, of course, but a process had commenced. Male workers in the rural villages of central Mexico learned how to make the trip north, how to cross without papers, and how to survive on the other side. They acquired—within the means of their modest incomes— American consumer tastes and returned annually to their villages in Michoacán or Jalisco with money in their jeans. With remitted earnings, it was said, one man could support four or five back home.[16]

What this meant, for one thing, was that Mexico and the United States shared a rural labor force, which both needed for agricultural development; more ominously, those laborers had acquired, by repeatedly crossing the border, an instinct for survival on the American side. As southwestern agro-business lost the pool of documented labor, it adjusted (and, indeed, welcomed) the parallel growth in the number of undocumented workers. As documented workers went in greater numbers into southwestern cities, they were in turn followed by greater numbers of undocumented laborers in the urban manufacturing enclaves of Los Angeles. To preserve this vital link between the southwestern economy and its alien labor pool, U.S. immigration authorities and the Border Patrol learned the art of "damage control." They adjusted their procedures and accommodated the needs of southwestern agro-business and manufacturing and an expanding southwestern middle class for a lettuce picker in the Imperial Valley or sewing machine operator in east Los Angeles or a maid or gardener in La Jolla.

Families in the rural villages of central Mexico learned to live much of the year without the man of the house, for he had gone north to pick lettuce or mow lawns. A few returned with enough money or with enough acquired skills to move up a notch or two demographically. But most simply continued their migratory habits. They would go to the farms of the U.S. Southwest or join the internal migration of rootless Mexican campesinos, people who had persisted in subsistence agriculture until the value of their meager production could not sustain their families. Then they would join the rural, propertyless migrants in the irrigated farmlands of the Mexican Northwest or would move to Monterrey or Guadalajara or Mexico City and begin consuming what they had formerly produced.

Mexico's official position on this issue—largely seconded by Mexican unions, industrialists, and large farm owners—was generally opposition to the loss of a labor force needed at home. The bracero program was the most visible reminder of Mexican economic dependence. No amount of official manipulation or distortion of statistics could conceal the fact that Mexican workers presumably vital to Mexican industry and agriculture had to go north to earn enough to feed their families. Furthermore, their employment in the United States was often uncertain, which in turn meant that if they did not get a job their families in central Mexico suffered. And, as Richard Craig pointed out in his study of the bracero program, the migrant returned with a few skills potentially useful to Mexican employers but also with much stronger notions about his worth and how little the Mexican political system had done for him. Mexican politicians in turn denounced as a national humiliation the competition of Mexicans for jobs as stoop laborers in a country where their religion and color made them the objects of racial slur.[17]

This was at first glance a curious interpretation of matters, given the views of southwestern agro-businessmen who preferred Mexican over domestic labor not only because the Mexican worked harder for less but because he was generally considered more reliable. In the early 1960s, however, the challenge to the program on the U.S. side grew stronger and more formidable. For one thing, organized labor, which had always opposed the importation of contract labor on the grounds that it lowered wage earnings for domestic workers, had a more sympathetic president to hear its complaint and a more aggressive secretary of labor to advance its cause in the bureaucracy. Unions also had new allies in the myriad social and religious reform groups—among them the National Council of Churches, the National Catholic Welfare Conference, the National Association for the Advancement of Colored People, and the National Consumers League—that called for "humane conditions" and a "living wage" in the vineyards of the Southwest.

In 1960 antibracero activists, armed with statistics readily supplied by the U.S. Department of Labor, narrowly failed to defeat a proposal to extend the program. Apparently Kennedy would have killed Public Law 78 in October 1961 but for a perception that without the law Mexico would not have permitted farm laborers to migrate to the U.S. Southwest for employment. The president was obviously aware of the grim reports on labor conditions on Southwest farms and certainly alert to the political clout of organized labor. But in signing the legislation that extended the program for another two years, he alluded to conditions in rural Mexico: "I am also aware of the serious impact in Mexico if many thousands of workers employed in this country were summarily deprived of this much-needed employment."[18]

Afterward, the Mexicans could no longer afford their customary ambivalence about this matter. As the opposition to the program grew in the United States, Mexican official statements over termination of Public Law 78 became more cautious. In August 1963 Sen. J. William Fulbright of Arkansas placed in the *Congressional Record* a statement from the Mexican ambassador,

Antonio Carillo Flores, who cited five reasons why the bracero program should not be abruptly ended. Among them was the frank admission of a modern reality in the U.S.–Mexican economic relationship: "It is not unexpected that the termination of an international agreement governing and regulating the rendering of service of Mexican workers will put an end to that type of seasonal migration; it is the effect or result of the migratory phenomenon. Therefore, the absence of an agreement would not end the problem but rather give rise to a de facto situation: the illegal introduction of Mexican workers into the United States."[19]

His appeal did not save the program from extinction the following year, but his words were prophetic. There were binding ties between two economies with vastly different political agendas. More important, the long debate over the bracero program had revealed something else about two diverse political cultures. It had stimulated a more profound assessment in Washington about rural domestic labor and, in Mexico, about the condition of what Octavio Paz, the famous Mexican philosopher and essayist, called the "other Mexico." Kennedy betrayed a political naiveté if he believed that retaining the opportunity of agricultural employment in the United States for Mexican field hands would resolve the disparity between rural and urban Mexico. In early 1964, as President Lyndon Johnson flew west to meet López on the border at Calexico, California, he carried with him a staff recommendation on the Alliance for Progress and the quality of life in rural Mexico. In response to middle-class criticism about the disparity between the quality of life in the countryside and the city and the more ominous statistics on marginal employment, López had announced that the Mexican government planned to create a corporation to manufacture and market inexpensive goods in rural Mexican villages. If successful, the report predicted, the program warranted application in other Latin American countries. But the Mexican president needed to be reminded that Cárdenas's notion of "each one, teach one" was inadequate for the needs of Mexico's rural peoples. They required college graduates to instruct them in the technical skills necessary for higher-paying jobs so they might earn the extra income to purchase the products of the new corporation.

Such an assessment, of course, hit squarely at Mexican economic policy after World War II. But the fact that the Mexican government did not dramatically shift course, using state authority to mitigate the social inequities that had accompanied the "Mexican miracle," is understandable. To have done so would have been an admission that the revolution had indeed failed to benefit its putative beneficiaries. More important, it would have required Mexican leaders to reduce their presence in the private sector and to expand their role as benefactors of campesinos and urban laborers. It would have required them to comport themselves as a supportive rather than a dominating force in a capitalist economy. They were prepared to share the power of economic decision with the business moguls in the private sector. They were not prepared to allow business to shape political decisions or to share power with PAN, known for its pro-business views.

The termination of the bracero agreement now made more urgent the long-range plans of the Mexican government for the economic and social transformation of the northern frontier. Such a project, Mexican leaders believed, would not only help to diversify the economies of northern Mexican cities but also to improve the image of frontier cities, which had acquired sordid reputations as bastions of saloons, brothels, and gambling houses. An early promoter of the border program was an ambitious *político*, Antonio Bermúdez, who had tried to clean up Juárez after World War II and then gone on to head up PEMEX. The best way to get rid of "Boys Town" (a favorite Texan sporting house), Bermúdez argued, was to make border cities such as Juárez more attractive to American tourists. And the border industrialization scheme provided the Mexicans with a much needed diversion from the heightening social and economic problems in the cities of central Mexico.

When the bracero program ended, however, northern cities such as Tijuana, Mexicali, and Juárez experienced sharp rises in unemployment. In Tijuana, for example, officials had a list of 50,000 braceros (many with families) waiting to cross over. Unable to do so, they joined the growing ranks of unemployed Mexicans on the frontier. For the government, they were not only an economic but, more important, a political problem. In Baja California the Democratic Electoral Front fashioned a coalition of Communists, farm workers, labor leaders, and disaffected PRI *políticos* (who had formed the Authentic Party of the Mexican Revolution) and challenged the government party in local elections.[20]

Clearly the government had to respond. The defiance in local politics even in faraway Baja California required the authoritative exercise of federal power. More problematic was finding a mechanism for controlling the army of migrant labor that had gathered in northern cities. But, in confronting this contingent, the Mexicans had sympathetic allies in Washington. In ending the bracero program, the U.S. government had dealt with one problem but in so doing had merely exacerbated a bigger problem for both Mexico and the United States. If angry Mexican workers denied legal admission into the United States decided to cross illegally, and if the Border Patrol could not— or Mexican authorities would not—stop them, there was little short of police state measures or a wall to keep them out.

The perceived solution was the Border Industrialization Program and the sprouting of *maquiladoras*—assembly plants for the U.S. garment, electronics, or toy industries—located in Mexico but producing for the U.S. market. Under the provisions of U.S. laws, they paid a tariff only on the value added to merchandise shipped to the United States, and they paid their employees in pesos not dollars. The benefits, the U.S. ambassador wrote later, were clear: "Mexico's Border Industrialization Program offers a notable opportunity for providing Mexicans with jobs and reducing the incentive for them to enter the United States as wetbacks. . . . The braceros returned to Mexico with some concept of our type of democracy, with a knowledge of modern agricultural methods, and with positive friendly feelings about the United States. Just the reverse is true of the wetbacks [180,000 of whom entered the United States in 1965]; they inevitably develop enmities toward the system that outlaws them and deports them."[21]

Such a view validated the Mexican saying that Americans require self-deception when they justify their support of economic programs on the grounds that these programs benefit Mexico more than the United States. But, in reality, Mexican officals had chosen to develop the border by integrating its northern cities into the U.S. economy. After 1965 they were able to boast that assembly plants had replaced brothels as the workplace for young *mexicanas*. And with the agreement guaranteeing Mexico a fixed percentage of Colorado River water and evidence of progress on controlling its salinity, they had a ready answer for critics who blamed them for advancing U.S. agro-business in the Imperial Valley and southwestern developers at the expense of Mexican farmers. Both Mexican and American leaders were aware of the potentially detrimental impact of border development on the region's fragile environment. Certainly, they were alert to the fact that the U.S. Southwest and the Mexican Northwest had limited water resources for agricultural development *on both sides of the border*. If agriculture on the Mexican side suffered—as, indeed, it did—they presumed that the *maquiladoras* and related manufacturing enterprises would compensate for the loss. The northern Mexico border towns would grow more rapidly than their counterparts on the American side, excepting El Paso and greater San Diego. Most important, the Mexican labor force now vital to the rapidly expanding consumer market in the U.S. Southwest would be stationed nearby. Mexicans would live and work in Mexico; they would cross over to the American side to purchase groceries or clothes.

Where both governments miscalculated, of course, was in their optimistic assumption that the *maquiladoras* would be able to employ Mexicans in sufficient numbers or that the rapidly expanding northern Mexico cities would be able to provide adequate social services. In 1966 there were 20 *maquiladoras* in northern Mexico cities. Four years later, there were 120, employing more than 20,000 workers, mostly young women. In comparison with their compatriots in the interior, residents of northern Mexico's border earned higher wages and were better educated, better fed, and better housed than their compatriots in the interior. Yet despite these advantages, the border residents in 1970 suffered with the populated regions of central Mexico in the diminished quality of social services and the growing number of unemployed or marginally employed men.[22]

Mexico's economic problems in the 1960s were too severe to be resolved even by a dynamic border economy. The policy of import substitution, deemed necessary for postwar industrial development, required a vigorous export sector in order to pay for the heavy imports of capital and intermediate goods and foreign investment, protection for the domestic producers of low-quality consumer goods, and, of course, low wages for workers. By the early 1960s Mexico had presumably arrived at the second stage of its postwar development; that is, a point where import substitution gave way to a more advanced economic strategy. Industry had reached the limits of its productivity; it had saturated its protected market with cheap durable goods that could not be sold in foreign markets. But Mexico lacked the technological capacity and skilled labor to shift to production of higher quality goods for its middle classes. The postwar increase of consumption had been greater than the increase in production. There was unemployment, a sharp increase in demand for imported goods, and only modest increases in the volume of exports. The combination of these meant that Mexicans were borrowing to finance consumption and that the government was unable to accommodate the work force displaced by the private sector.[23]

The Border Industrialization Program neither revitalized the Mexican economy nor provided adequate employment for those young Mexicans who had grown up during the "economic miracle." Its creators' intent was, at bottom, political: Mexico's beleaguered *políticos* in the 1960s *required* the supportive link with the U.S. economy because they knew American leaders were more committed to Mexican economic development than to the resolution of its concomitant social inequities. Knowing these priorities, they also correctly inferred that the U.S. government would be more tolerant of their forceful exercise of power in preserving the political system they had created. In a brilliantly orchestrated political strategy, they had diverted hemispheric attention from their failures as revolutionary heirs. They had done this by posturing themselves as defenders of self-determination and nonintervention in the OAS, yet they had not, as had other hemispheric nations, suffered American economic retaliation. They had not bowed before the U.S. political presence in hemispheric diplomatic battles. International humiliation to Washington was unnecessary. Theirs was a much craftier strategy. They had permitted—indeed, abetteed—the subordinating of the Mexican economy to the U.S. economy. They had used economic ties to remind the American government that it had no realistic alternative to the political system they had created.

chapter 5

TROUBLED NEIGHBORS

Nineteen sixty-eight began as a year of triumphant expectation for Mexico. Lauded by European and American leaders for its economic achievement, the nation now gained an honor unique in Latin America. The International Olympic Committee had selected Mexico City as the site for the summer games. It was a signal triumph for the government, and Mexico's leaders gloried in their accomplishments. President Gustavo Díaz Ordaz declared his nation stable, prosperous, and united, a sentiment echoed not only by the government's political minions but dutifully repeated by the national media. Leaders of Mexico's labor unions and peasant organizations, who represented millions of Mexicans largely bypassed in this "economic miracle," nonetheless remained loyal. The state, they said, had brought harmony between capital and labor.

Rarely did the government require the use of its own forces to beat down fractious unions, for its loyal constituency of labor leaders performed that task. Nor did it need censorship to intimidate the press; it suborned newspaper and magazine publishers by supplying their newsprint and purchasing two-thirds of the advertising that appeared in their publications. Occasionally, an intellectual dissident—the essayist Octavio Paz, the novelist Carlos Fuentes—penned a critique that stripped away the pretentiousness of the regime and exposed its inner life. But most writers were unable to survive on their writings and, ultimately, came to depend on a government they vilified to provide a slot in the bloated bureaucracy or a low-paying position at the university. Those who retained intellectual honesty and wrote critically about the excessive display of wealth or crass opportunism sometimes found

66

themselves praised and rewarded by a government that needed dissenters to prove it was tolerant of dissent.[1]

None of the revolutionary rhetoric about the "Mexican miracle" was able to mitigate the social travesty embodied in statistics on family income distribution: from 1950 the top 10 percent of middle- and upper-class families *increased* its share of national income from 60 percent to 64 percent. And it was from the children of these beneficiaries that the challenge emanated, which made the protests of 1968 all the more galling to Mexico's leaders. They had been able to persuade the lower classes that they did not deserve what few social benefits they received. Those who had gotten more because the lower classes had gotten less were outraged.

There were limits to the government's tolerance, especially if critics went beyond verbal denunciations of the failure of Mexico's leaders to fulfill the revolutionary promise and challenged their credibility, their inherited claim on power. By 1968 they were more or less resigned to the fact that the putative beneficiaries of the "economic miracle"—the middle classes— neither loved nor admired them. But they presumed the discontented middle-class Mexican, after reflection on what might happen to his standard of living if the government did indeed address the needs of the "other Mexico," would tolerate their retention of political power. After all, Mexico's revolutionary chieftains and its modern political elite came largely from the middle class. Postrevolutionary Mexico had developed in the reformist capitalist tradition that had encouraged upward social mobility by the lower middle classes, noticeably diminished the role of the upper classes, and introduced benevolent measures for labor and campesinos.

Within this captive sector of the revolutionary "family," Mexico's leaders were prepared, as they had in the past, to placate disgruntled unionists with a bribe, employment in one of the myriad government agencies, or a few acres of worthless land. Out in the countryside, of course, they were ready to use force to subdue the defiant, in the tradition of Spain's colonial viceroys. But the success of these tactics depended on preserving the mystique of the "good leader," who may act benevolently or repressively but always with the intention of maintaining unity in his "family," whose members, regardless of their social or economic status, look ultimately to him for strength and not to one another. Emiliano Zapata, Alvaro Obregón, and Pancho Villa had set the standard for the revolutionary cult of personality, Plutarro Elías Calles had brilliantly played the part of *jefe máximo,* and Lázaro Cárdenas had reaffirmed ordinary Mexicans' innate faith in the firm but benevolent leader. None of his successors was able to generate the admiration and affection he commanded among Mexicans. Miguel Alemán had the look of a clubbable businessman who could be trusted to guide Mexico's economic development along the right path but could not be trusted with the national treasury. Ruiz Cortines was a mild-mannered avuncular man who proved less tolerant of government thievery. Adolfo López Mateos was energetic and likable and believed the Mexican people loved him because his lackeys told him they did. When he discovered they had lied, he flew into a rage.

Diaz Ordaz had little of López's contrived affability. Worse, he did not look presidential. He was not handsome and did not inspire his people. But he had a single-minded determination, the will to exercise executive power if challenged, and a disinclination to compromise. In 1965, after a violent clash between rivalrous groups in the National Peasant Confederation left 30 dead, Díaz compelled the head of the union to resign his post. He fired the head of PRI, Carlos Madrazo, in a dispute over democratic standards in local elections; removed the director of Mexico's social security administration, who had been looking into corruption within the system; and was so enraged over the National Autonomous University's tolerance of student demonstrators that he demanded the resignation of that institution's president.

Calles had ruled firmly, but Calles had possessed credibility. And he had exercised power in a Mexico that was in many ways still premodern, when Mexicans looked to their presidents to lead the nation into an uncertain future. In 1968 they no longer believed their political leaders had that vision or, indeed, the capability to address the problems of modernity. Díaz Ordaz confirmed their fears. As the protests spread from within the governmental family into other segments of Mexican society, he grew more defensive and, ultimately, more repressive. Student protests over electoral frauds in Sonora and Yucatán brought not an investigation but a police crackdown on the protestors.

But the outbursts of August, September, and October of 1968—remembered by *chilangos* (as Mexico City residents are called) as "Tlatelolco," the area where the bloodiest confrontation took place—were the most serious challenge to the government since the late 1920s, when Cristeros defied Calles. Kenneth Johnson, a perceptive analyst of Mexican politics, has described Tlatelolco as "urban jacquerie, a people's uprising, against a central authority perceived as cruel and uncaring. Organized, and sometimes armed, university students became the voices for interpreting and articulating that which the masses could not articulate for themselves."[2] Students at Mexico City's National Autonomous University (UNAM), located near the site for the enormous Sports Palace the government was building to house Olympic events, denounced the project. It was yet another reminder that millions of Mexicans (themselves included) could see the building but could not afford to attend the Olympic Games.

Student protests became more than an irritant, and the mayor, beholden to the president, resolved to demonstrate that the government had no intention of allowing the students to disrupt completion of the Sports Palace. Thus, in late July, when police received a routine call from a harassed principal of a private high school to settle a fight between his students and those of a nearby vocational school, the mayor dispatched 200 grenadiers to subdue them. Middle-class Mexicans were shocked by the heavy-handed style of the grenadiers to deal with the situation. A few days later, students from the National Federation of Technical Students (one of the many subgroups in PRI) asked for permission to hold a march on 26 July (a day of celebration in Cuba that is often commemorated by Latin American Communists) to demand the resignation of Mexico City's police chief. More than 3,000 students swarmed into the Zócalo, the large square adjacent to the National Palace. Following several incendiary speeches and confrontations, the police dispersed them. The government threw the head of Mexico's Communist party and seven employees of the newspaper *La Voz de México* in jail. The next day another crowd of students gathered, demanding their release.

The government responded by incarcerating student leaders. It now confronted a threat far more menacing than an isolated labor strike or peasant land seizure. Its authority had been challenged. To grant concessions under protest would be to acknowledge the failure not only of its ability to keep order but also of its economic program from the late 1940s. The protestors may have been middle class in origin and certainly in aspiration, but they voiced their demands in the revolutionary promise of democracy and social justice. Mexico's postwar leaders, in their crassness and political opportunism, had forsaken that promise, using as pretext the specious argument that Mexico could not have economic development *and* equity. By 1968 it was clear that the nation had reached a turning point. Economic inequities had worsened; industry and agriculture had stagnated; foreign commerce had suffered; poverty had not only persisted but had become more strikingly visible in the cities. A generation had come of age and was without hope for a brighter future unless fundamental changes were made. Mexico needed modern leaders with the imagination of some of their predecessors, leaders able to demonstrate their faith in the Mexican revolutionary promise. What Mexico required was democracy.[3]

Confronting a broader coalition of student groups on the Left, the government began hastily putting together its own army of counter-protestors. A national Strike Committee (representing a combined student population of 160,000 at UNAM and the National Polytechnic Institute) presented a list of demands framed in such provocative language to the government's authority that the interior (Gobernación) Secretary, Luis Echeverría, as they had anticipated, peremptorily rejected them. Echeverría, already being mentioned as Díaz's probable successor, could ill afford to show mercy. The law school faculty and student body at UNAM began dispatching runners with denunciatory broadsides into Mexico City's poorer neighborhoods. Echeverría announced that he would meet privately with them to discuss their grievances; they demanded a public airing. This, of course, was out of the question, and when the Strike Committee summoned workers, students, small-business owners, and even a few parents for yet another demonstration in the spacious plaza of the Zócalo, Echeverría organized a counter-demonstration of government workers. Embarrassingly, some of them joined the opposition in their denunciations of government misrule. When the protestors occupied the ancient cathedral and raised the North Vietnamese flag, they were denounced as Communists. In the dead of night on 28 August, Mexican troops forcibly removed them.

Díaz had to justify such harsh measures. Mexican presidents have considerable power in such situations, but they cannot exercise that power with impunity. Díaz chose the presidential state of the union address (given on 1 September of every year) to explain the extraordinary measures the police and military had been compelled to take: "The situation has reached the point where methods of expression have been grossly abused," and, as president, he said he had the constitutional obligation to preserve public order. The students intended to disrupt the Olympic Games, thus denying all Mexicans the "legitimate satisfaction" of hosting the first Olympiad in a Spanish-speaking country. He was willing to extend more autonomy to the educational institutions, most of them already under the de facto control of striking students, but, in an ambiguously worded concession, questioned if the Mexican congress should set aside its sedition laws: "Should it not be considered a crime to affect our national sovereignty, endangering the territorial integrity of the republic in compliance with the dictates of a foreign goverment [Cuba]? If it [the subversion law] is abolished, no crime will have a political character. Is that what is desired?"[4] The last remark merely served to inspire the students to launch yet another protest and demands for dialogue. Echeverría responded on 18 September by ordering 10,000 troops to the spacious UNAM campus, which a major newspaper had declared was staging area for a strike against the Sports Palace.

The Strike Committee quickly moved its operations to the Polytechnic Institute in the northern part of the city, but within a few days it was obvious that the *organized* antigovernment coalition was distintegrating. In its wake came another wave of protest, disorganized, anarchical, and randomly destructive. The bands seized transit buses and set them afire. They threw up barricades. Not since the violent days of the revolution had *chilangos* experienced such fears. The government appeared helpless in containing it. Then, as quickly as it had erupted, the violence ended.

But the social conflict had not been resolved. The government now perceived the cumulative protests that had rocked the capital for more than a month as a crisis of authority. There were rumors of yet another gathering, this one at the Plaza de Tres Culturas to the north in Tlatelolco, near the foreign relations ministry and a rabbit warren of pastel apartment buildings occupied mostly by middle-class Mexicans. At Tlatelolco the Aztecs had made their last stand against the conquering Spaniards. On 1 October the police invaded one of the buildings and arrested two Guatemalan terrorists, who, it was announced, had told them that antigovernment students were using apartments in the compound to organize.

The Strike Committee, responding to this provocation, first called for a march at Tlatelolco then, learning that Mexican troops had taken positions in the area, just as quickly reversed itself. Ordinary Mexicans have little respect for the police, but they rightly fear the military, and in tense situations soldiers might use their weapons against unarmed civilians. But committee leaders did approve the notion of a public meeting, and 4,000 Mexicans (many of them women and children) gathered in the dusk to listen as fiery speakers exhorted them to "unite and take the city." Police and military surrounded them, virtually blockading the area with armor. The frightened civilians now heard shouts from the speakers urging them to remain peaceful and orders from policemen with bullhorns to disperse.

When they refused the riot-control squads moved in, thrashing with their clubs. The police found themselves attacked by angry civilians, among them youths crazed by having drunk a murderous concoction of rum, tequila, and the drug cyclopal. The police began firing their weapons. From the upper floors of one of the nearby buildings, an alleged gathering place for Strike Committee leaders, came rifle shots. The police departed, and a battalion of paratroopers, reinforced with mortars, armor, and a helicopter, suddenly appeared. The helicopter dropped eerie green flares. There was a futile appeal to the crowd from the commanding general, but the moment he began to speak the guerrillas opened fire from the nearby buildings, and he fell to the ground. For nine hours Tlatelolco was a grim spectacle of bloody confrontation between a government and its people. Soldiers fired randomly at the fleeing. From the Tlatelolco cinema came terrified moviegoers who were beaten and shot by the roving soldiers. A few tried to escape the melee by climbing to the ledges of buildings but were felled by machinegun fire. By morning the troops had pacified the area.

Tlatelolco's exact death toll may never be known. The government announced that there were 200 casualties, but there were doubtless many more, perhaps as many as 1,000. Nor did Mexicans believe that the military had acted in self-defense. In truth, both the government and the opposition wanted this confrontation. Tlatelolco suited both as a battle zone. From its surrounding buildings, the snipers were able to fire on the gathering troops below as they were shooting and beating innocent Mexicans, most of whom had gathered to protest the abuse of power. The Strike Committee knew how the president would react to this latest challenge; his defense minister later confirmed that he was under orders to suppress what Díaz called an uprising.[5]

To most Americans the most lingering memory of the 1968 Olympics was the raised fists of two black athletes on the victors' platform. But for a generation of expectant Mexicans, inspired by the reformist youth movements that shook Western governments, Tlatelolco served as reminder of the old Mexico, its idols and myths and a political structure that was fractured but not broken by the rupture. No Western government challenged by student rebellion, save Mexico's, had responded with such force. In their defiance, Mexico's youth had shown the world to what violent extremes the nation's leaders would go. The uprising had failed, but its participants were profoundly changed by the experience. In their later rise to positions of influence within government, universities, political parties, and business, the experience ultimately gave them credibility, if not control of the seat of power. None of Díaz's successors—not even Luis Echeverría, whom Díaz "tapped" as president in 1970—could ignore the legacy of Tlatelolco.[6]

Nor could the U.S. government ignore the impact of Mexico's economic and political crisis for the situation on the border, particularly in the lower Rio Grande Valley in Texas. Outspoken Mexican Americans, many of whom had begun calling themselves Chicanos, had already made the impoverished condition of Mexican rural labor in the Southwest a political issue. In a meeting with Díaz a year before Tlatelolco, President Lyndon Johnson spoke expansively about border development to reporters but privately expressed his displeasure over the growing number of illegal entries. The problem was especially acute in Texas, where militant Chicanos, determined to unionize the Mexican laborers in the Rio Grande Valley, confronted farmers who began hiring undocumented workers to break the strike and counted on Texas Rangers to back them. Clearly, the chairman of the Inter-Agency Commission on Mexican-American Affairs reminded the president, Johnson could not afford to remain silent on this matter. He urged the president to persuade Texas governor John Connally, an LBJ protégé, to withdraw the rangers quietly. He reminded Johnson that most Mexican Americans supported his Vietnam policy (Hispanics, in fact, were the most decorated ethnic group in the Vietnam War). Indeed, the chairman concluded, the "language and culture of the Mexican America" was a "national asset" in U.S. relations with Latin America.[7]

Such words were of little consolation to a U.S. president confronting in the Chicano movement yet another separatist movement in the fragmenting Democratic coalition. In the labor struggles of the Rio Grande Valley of Texas and especially in the farm workers' movement in California, Chicano activists confronted the alliance of agro-business, state government, and the U.S Department of Agriculture, which skillfully and callously exploited the availability of legal and illegal Mexican labor to beat them back. In the upper Rio Grande Valley of New Mexico, they found a cause in the "land grant" wars and a champion, Reies López Tijerina, who founded the Federal Alliance of Land Grants. (The alliance's immediate goal was the recovery of lands fraudulently taken by Anglos in the aftermath of the Mexican–American War, but the inspiration was the creation of Aztlán, an independent community of collective farms. Ultimately, their tactics, which included the temporary occupation of the Kit Carson National Forest in 1966 and a much-publicized raid on the Rio Arriba County Courthouse the following year, brought down upon the alliance the wrath of federal and state authorities.)

López Tijerina eventually wound up in jail, but his cause struck a responsive chord among Chicanos. Throughout the Southwest, especially in Texas, they began to organize politically. In Crystal City, Texas, they took over the local city government in 1967. Within a few years, the Anglos regrouped and regained power. But the character of southwestern political culture—expressed in the myriad Chicano political organizations, legal support groups (such as the Mexican American Legal Defense Fund and Mexican mutual aid societies), the political activism of southwestern middle-class Hispanics (best symbolized in the mayoral victory of Henry Cisneros in San Antonio), and the extension of the voting rights act to include southwestern minorities—was unalterably changed. Chicanos had not yet begun to call themselves "Mexicans," but the "Mexican connection" was present everywhere—in the revolutionary graffiti exhorting young Chicanos to emulate Zapata or Villa and rise against their oppressors; in the calls for unity with the captive army of laborers in the *maquiladoras* or the migratory bands of illegals crossing the border; in the pilgrimages to the Shrine of the Virgin of Guadalupe; in the demands for bilingualism and a curriculum that stressed cultural awareness among Mexican Americans. Ambitious young Mexican American politicians in Texas and California gained leverage in both parties, especially the Democratic party, by reminding Anglos of the political dangers it boded.

Chicano activists and the Mexican generation of '68 may not have had a common cause, but in their reaffirmation of "Mexicanness" they reminded both countries of cultural links. Both groups had managed to jar the leaders of both governments from their complacency about the social and political legacy defined by intertwined economies. Officials in the United States diminished the appeal of Chicano separatism by invoking federal laws—among them the Bilingual Education Act and the Voting Rights Act—and both political parties, especially the Republicans, stepped up their campaigns to add more Mexican American voters. These and similar efforts validated the nation's political traditions and professed cultural pluralism. However laudatory, these reforms had a political purpose—to divert American public attention from the binding and presumably lasting economic bonds with Mexico, symbolized by the continuing U.S. dependence on Mexican labor and the U.S. economic penetration of Mexico.

It was the U.S. economic presence that reminded Mexican leaders of the concessions they had made to American companies and investors to bring about the "Mexican miracle" and of their political vulnerability for having debased the nation's sovereignty in the process. For Echeverría, undoing those economic ties was unthinkable. To do nothing, however, posed a political risk. What was necessary, then, was a series of diversionary tactics, which Echeverría began even before assuming office. In his presidential campaign, he broke with tradition by distancing himself from Díaz Ordaz and calling for a new Mexican internationalism. Echeverría the mastermind of the Tlatelolco "massacre" was suddenly and visibly transformed into Echeverría the populist and nationalist. Such rhetoric inspired those Mexican nationalists who had long decried the nation's loss of real sovereignty and attributed it to the U.S. economic presence. If Mexico's foreign *economic* policy became more aggres-

Mexican President Miguel Alemán's motorcade down Pennsylvania Avenue, April 1947. Courtesy *Archivo General de la Nación*

Presidents Dwight D. Eisenhower and Adolfo Ruiz Cortines dedicate the Falcon Dam on the Rio Grande, October 1953. Courtesy *Archivo General de la Nación*

Irrigated farmland in Sonora, 1961. Photo by Kip Ross. Courtesy National Geographic Society

Teacher reading to pupils as school is built in rural Mexico, 1961. Photo by Kip Ross. Courtesy National Geographic Society

Presidents John F. Kennedy and Adolfo López Mateos, Mexico City, July 1962. Courtesy Archivo General de la Nación

Presidents Lyndon B. Johnson and Gustavo Díaz Ordaz in Ciudad Juárez, October 1967, after signing Chamizal agreement. Photo by Wilbur E. Garrett. Courtesy National Geographic Society

Student protest at Plaza de Tres Culturas, Mexico City, 1968. Courtesy *Archivo General de la Nación*

Presidents Jimmy Carter and José López Portillo, Mexico City, February 1979. Courtesy *Jimmy Carter Library*

sive, they argued, the nation would be able to afford the inevitable economic liabilities of reducing the U.S. economic presence and redefining what Americans called a "special relationship." President Richard Nixon, perhaps unintentionally, aggravated the political situation by twin decisions made without consulting the Mexican government: "Operation Intercept," the momentary shutdown of the border in June 1969, part of Nixon's highly publicized and largely ineffectual drug interdiction program, and the 1971 import tax surcharge, which severely affected a country that sent 70 percent of its exports to the United States.[8]

The internal political adjustment, Mexico's "democratic opening," which meant greater tolerance of public criticism, less interference in the universities, and strengthening of opposition parties, to cite a few examples, mitigated some of the bitterness of Tlatelolco. It was, moreover, within the revolutionary tradition. But Echeverría's foreign policy marked a new adventurousness for Mexico that, some feared, would lead to greater complications with Washington. True, previous Mexican leaders, notably Carranza during World War I and Cárdenas in the late 1930s, had brazenly defied the United States, but they had done so at a time when American leaders had become preoccupied with greater menaces to U.S. security elsewhere. Echeverría planned to deviate from Washington's international agenda; he intended to make Mexico a leader in third world politics and a guiding force in the New Industrial Economic Order.

With détente and the reality of a multipolar world, his arguments were persuasive. With the end of the "special relationship," the new Mexican internationalism seemed inevitable. If Mexico could not depend on the U.S. market to sell Mexican products it would have to diversify its trade patterns, not only in Latin America but with countries theretofore insignificant for Mexican exporters. Increased trade would bring about new trading partners and new sources of investment, credit, and technology. From 1971 until 1975 Echeverría embarked on trips to 37 countries—among them the Soviet Union, Cuba, and the Peoples Republic of China—and significantly expanded the number of diplomatic missions. In 1971 the Mexican president proclaimed before the U.N. General Assembly Mexico's conversion to third world internationalism and in the following year proposed a Charter of Economic Rights and Duties of States.

As if to flaunt his defiance of the United States, Echeverría—at considerable political risk—cultivated the socialist leader of Chile, Salvador Allende, whose policies had brought down upon Chile the wrath of the Nixon administration. When the U.S. economic blockade of Chile cut Allende off from traditional sources of credit, Mexico offered loans and, later, provided wheat and petroleum in years when the country no longer had sufficient reserves. When Allende was killed in a military coup in September 1973, Mexico became a haven for Chilean exiles and—in a noticeable departure from its international stance on recognition—cut diplomatic ties with the government of Augusto Pinochet, the right-wing general who led the coup against Allende.

When the oil embargo commenced, neither Mexico, which was not a member of the Organization of Petroleum Exporting Countries (OPEC), nor Venezuela (a founding member) went along with the Arab producers. Despite their reluctance, Congress, in a fit over the issue, retaliated against Venezuela by withdrawing preferential trade treatment. Already, President Carlos Andrés Pérez of Venezuela and Echeverría had begun promoting a new Latin American economic system (SELA) that excluded the United States but included Cuba, which had strengthened its economic and cultural links with other Latin American countries. Latin American governments formally approved SELA in 1974. In the same year, the Mexicans were in the vanguard of the movement for reforms in the OAS, one of which permitted member states the freedom to restore diplomatic relations with Havana.[9]

Mexico undertook bold new measures directed at multinational corporations. One was the 1972 Law on the Registration of Technology Transfer and the Use and Exploitation of Patents and Trademarks, the other the 1973 Law to Promote Mexican Investment and Regulate Foreign Investment. The latter required "Mexicanization" of selected companies by stipulating that Mexicans must own 51 percent of the stock in such concerns. In addition, the Mexican government in a unilateral decision declared a 200-mile maritime economic zone to safeguard its marine resources. Thus by 1973 the government controlled petroleum, the railroads, telegraph communications, electricity, and petrochemical industries; required 100 percent Mexican ownership of radio and television, overland transport, natural gas distribution, and banks and financial institutions; and imposed severe restrictions on Mexican fisheries and marine processors, mining, basic chemicals, secondary petrochemicals, rubber, iron and steel manufacturing, cement, glass, fertilizers, cellulose, aluminum, publishing, soft drinks, film, and urban, maritime, and air transportation.[10]

These measures challenged but did not break the American economic grip. In 1970, a Mexican economist calculated, foreign (mostly American) enterprises controlled almost half of the major industrial firms, and foreign capital was concentrated in the most rapidly expanding economic sectors—capital and basic intermediate goods, American multinationals dominated the automotive industry (57 percent), rubber (76 percent), mining and metallurgy (54 percent), nonelectrical machinery (52 percent), transportation equipment (64 percent), computers and office equipment (88 percent), copper and aluminum (72 percent), tobacco (100 percent), chemicals and pharmaceuticals (86 percent), and commerce (53 percent). Moreover, two-thirds of U.S. multinational investment lay in capital- rather than labor-intensive sectors of the economy. The law of 1973 affected most of these but did not noticeably reduce the foreign hold. Automobile industries—Ford, Chrysler, General Motors, and Volkswagen—remained 100 percent foreign-owned, as did Kodak, Sears, and Dow Chemical. Mexicanization, in many instances, provided yet another means for foreign investors to shield themselves from retaliation. For a price, many Mexicans were willing to lend their names to permit circumvention of legal restrictions on foreign participation. In an unanticipated way, Mexicanization also provided safeguards against expropriation and greater access to Mexican financial lending institutions.[11]

Echeverría intended to shift Mexico from its presumably unshakable fixation on relations with the United States or, in other words, to "politicize" Mexican foreign policy. But the results of his new internationalism were often ambiguous. For example, in 1975 he reversed a long-standing Mexican opposition to Guatemala's claim to a portion of Belize (formerly British Honduras), which had gained independence in 1970. The announcement eased tensions with Guatemala but predictably exacerbated relations between that country and Belize, which called on the retiring British to dispatch troops and arms for its protection. When Echeverría tried to placate both sides, Mexico's momentary reconciliation with Guatemala took a turn for the worse, and Mexico's global image suffered. Shortly afterward, the Mexican foreign minister to Guatemala resigned.

A more aggressive and independent foreign policy could not distract from the structural weaknesses of the Mexican economy or its seemingly irreversible integration into the U.S. economy. In the six years of the Echeverría presidency, the nation's trade deficit grew from $1 billion to $3 billion, the foreign debt quintupled to $20 billion, and the dependence on American investments and markets held steady. In the last year of his *sexenio*, the deteriorating economic situation on the border, where the *maquiladoras* laid off 32,000 laborers, directly affected the interior Mexican economy. In Mexico City's Federal District 500,000 workers lost their jobs and 3,000 small companies declared bankruptcy. To stave off disaster for small farm owners, the government permitted the price of beans and tortillas (staples in the poor Mexican's diet) to escalate by more than 250 percent, but the effect of the decision was to malnourish the poor. In a desperate populist gesture, Echeverría proudly announced yet another law to regulate foreign investment and the expropriation of private large farms in Sonora, twin declarations that accelerated capital flight and precipitated a financial crisis.

These economic shocks unleashed yet another wave of social protest. This outburst, though not as destructive as the uprising of 1968, had more serious political implications, for its leaders sprang from a renegade branch of the Confederation of Mexican Workers, the Democratic Tendency. In fall 1975 this group sponsored a protest march of 250,000 in the capital, and in the following year its electrical workers defied the PRI a second time by organizing students, urban squatters, and peasants into the National Front of Labor, Peasant, and Popular Insurgency.[12] This new bloc, wrote James Cockcroft, "represented a more serious threat to the state than did the student-led mass mobilizations of 1968, because now industrial workers were in the forefront."[13]

Since 1958, when López Mateos spoke passionately about addressing the social inequities spawned by Mexico's uneven distribution of wealth, a disquieting ritual had taken in every presidential succession. López Mateos had inherited a social crisis, failed to resolve it, and passed it along to his successor, who in turn had begun his *sexenio* with eloquent professions of commitment to fulfill the revolutionary promise, remarks usually qualified with somber reminders about the imperative of economic growth to pay for it. Nineteen seventy-six, when José López Portillo took office, was not much different, save for the alacrity with which the new president took on the assignment. And he was prepared to make concessions—first to the International Monetary Fund, which required in return for a $1.2 billion emergency loan a slashing of federal spending, limits on wage increases, and easing of restrictions on credit and currency exchange policies; then to the harassed opposition, particularly the Partido Acción Nacional, which had boycotted the 1976 election to protest Mexico's endemic political corruption. Under the political reforms of 1977, minority opposition parties were guaranteed a minimum number of seats in the Chamber of Deputies, the Communist party regained legal status, and the government agreed to allow registered political parties an opportunity to voice their concerns on television.

Such concessions eased the political tensions that had lingered since Tlatelolco. Accompanying them were even more heartening reports about Mexico's economic future. In 1976 the government had announced the finding of geologists that southern Mexico and the Bay of Campeche contained vast oil reserves. The news electrified the nation. Since 1917, when Article 27 of the Mexican Constitution proudly declared that the subsoil wealth of the nation belonged to the people, ordinary Mexicans have retained a simple yet admirable conviction that the oil underneath *their* soil was indeed *theirs*. Calles had defended that principle; Cárdenas had gallantly reaffirmed it. Now, in the midst of a grave economic and social crisis, their leaders informed them that Mexico was rich. The nation's international economic and political standing would be restored.

In the six years following the discovery, oil production expanded by 300 percent, estimates of Mexico's reserves in 1983 increased 1200 percent from calculations in the early 1970s, and the nation became the fourth largest oil producer in the world. There were glowing predictions of another "Mexican miracle." Unlike the economic model of the postwar years, when Mexico's leaders had developed manufacturing with monies from agricultural exports, the nation now had the capacity to modernize by using oil exports to get hard currency and credit from abroad. Mexico went into a veritable frenzy of development. PEMEX, the national petroleum company, became a "state within a state," a mountainous bureaucracy of corruption and power. In the South its operations transformed sleepy communities into boomtowns and drove hundreds of small farm owners and campesinos from their lands. But they were forgotten casualties in the impressive statistics of these years: from 1974 to 1982 oil's share of export earnings jumped from 4 percent to 75 percent, and foreign investment increased by 500 percent in three years (1978–80). Mexico enjoyed a phenomenal 8 percent annual growth rate from 1978 to 1981 and created a million new jobs every year.[14]

Oil wealth—real and symbolic—not only reinforced Mexico's pretensions as third world leader but persuaded López Portillo and his coterie that they might conveniently disregard early warnings about what petroleum wealth could and could not do for a developing nation. The cautionary advice was both foreign and domestic in its provenance. President Pérez of Venezuela had visited Mexico before López's inauguration and warned, "The ideal [policy] for a country with petroleum must be to produce neither more nor less than what can be intelligently used for the development of the country."[15] In 1978, as the president exalted in his role as leader of an economy run amuck with development projects, a distinguished group of academics and engineers gathered at the College of Mexico to express their disappointment over his policies, especially his apparently unquenchable faith that petroleum sales would revitalize the Mexican economy. The historian Olga Pellicer offered the most devastating rebuttal: "In history there have been no countries that have been capable of overcoming structural dependence while increasing their exports of natural resources."[16]

Dependence in Mexico is a word laden with political implications and is used almost exclusively in reference to Mexico's economic bondage to the United States. López shared his predecessor's pride in Mexico's new international status and gloried in the political and economic windfalls that accompanied the petroleum discoveries. And he was certainly mindful of how Mexico's oil wealth would affect relations with the United States, especially in years when the Arab oil boycott had raised new fears of U.S. dependence on foreign oil sources. López reasoned correctly that the petroleum discoveries in Mexico enhanced his nation's *strategic* value to its meddlesome northern neighbor and provided Mexico with considerable bargaining power on other issues. Yet, paradoxically, if Mexico agreed to sell its petroleum (and natural gas) to the Americans, then Mexican dependence would not be lessened but magnified.

President Jimmy Carter, who took the presidential oath less than two months after López, gave Mexican affairs an urgency unparalleled in U.S. foreign policy since Woodrow Wilson in 1913. In February 1977 Carter received his Mexican counterpart in Washington, intending to help a neighbor regain its credit rating in the international financial community and to express his genuine concern for some of Mexico's problems. In this encounter, Carter, who speaks Spanish, was apparently successful in blending his instinctive compassion for the underdog and engineer's precision in detailing areas of concern. In the end, however, the joint communiqué, as Robert Pastor has written, reflected the Mexican penchant for vagueness in such public statements rather than the American preoccupation for clarity: " 'The two Presidents pledged that they would examine closely in the next few months the multiple aspects of the relations between Mexico and the United States with a view to developing policies that reflected the interrelated nature of mutual problems.' This was López Portillo's formulation of the problem; Carter's proposed solution was a consultative mechanism of cabinet ministers from both governments to examine the full gamut of issues and report to the two Presidents."[17]

Thus began Carter's entry into what Pastor has appropriately named the "circular illogic" in the U.S.–Mexican relationship. As the two leaders broached the various issues that divided their governments and made tentative gestures to resolve them, they were confronted with the energy question, which was for both a political issue. López had to find a way for Mexico to benefit from its oil and natural gas wealth without appearing humble before the menacing American giant; Carter had to demonstrate resolve in securing U.S. access to Mexico's petroleum without conveying weakness. López announced that Mexico would construct a natural gas pipeline north to the United States; the Mexican Left denounced him on the grounds that it was preferable to burn off the natural gas in Mexico than give it to the gringos. (The fact that the gas would be sold did not shake their conviction that the decision was dishonorable.) Carter genuinely tried to show his sensitivity for Mexican nationalism. Asked if he would insist on Mexican sales of natural gas to the United States, he responded that the United States would purchase only what the Mexicans wished to sell.

The ensuing public controversy over this matter clouded U.S.–Mexican relations throughout the Carter administration and persuaded many observers that Carter and López did not get along well, though their personal meetings were for the most part cordial and productive. Mexico and the United States have a common fear of national insecurity, yet because neither government can give that fear a common definition, no American or Mexican president dares risk showing too much trust in his counterpart lest it be interpreted as weakness. And there are the unavoidable domestic political intrusions into the diplomatic agenda. When Carter learned that private U.S. natural gas companies were negotiating with PEMEX to purchase gas at a price considered too high by the administration, energy advisor James Schlesinger told the Mexican director of PEMEX, Jorge Díaz Serrano, that his government wanted an agreement but considered the offer of the private U.S. companies too high. If Mexico went ahead, he warned, the natural gas companies would use the deal as a means of pressuring Congress to permit an escalation of domestic gas and fuel oil prices. Schlesinger even dispatched a team to Mexico City to reinforce his warning, but PEMEX officials ignored it by signing a preliminary agreement with six private U.S. natural gas firms. Upset, Carter invited López to Washington to participate in the signing of the Panama Canal treaties, but López declined on the grounds that the ceremony conflicted with his annual state of the union address and that the treaties did not sufficiently express Panamanian sovereignty.

López Portillo was already beset by problems with the proposed pipeline. In August 1977 he met with a delegation whose members expressed strong reservations about his oil policy and the recurring fears of Mexican dependence. Mexico, López assured them, would retain a necessary amount of its oil wealth for internal development. It was not dependent on U.S. purchases of its oil and natural gas. With the latter, there were only two choices—burn it or sell it. Later, in a session with PEMEX officials, another persistent critic, Heberto Padilla, told that Mexico was in a "position of force" on this matter, blurted, "Certainly, there is a position of force, and the Americans have it. Mexico is economically dependent on them. . . . If Mexico now sends 70% of its exports to the United States, the sale of oil and gas will increase that dependence to 86%. How does this give us a position of force?" With that the exchange escalated into mutual fault finding, a not uncommon habit of Mexicans where the "American question" is at issue. Padilla rambled on about the humiliation of Mexico's territorial losses, the Veracruz intervention of 1914, Panama, Guantánamo, Puerto Rico, and Vietnam. When he finally finished, PEMEX magnate Díaz Serrano said, "The United States is no longer the imperial power of yesteryear. There are no more invasions. [And] just as the Panama Canal was built by Americans with American money, the gas pipeline will be constructed by Mexicans with Mexican money."[18]

It was a fitting response to an emotional Mexican nationalist, but in the offing the deal fell through. Increasingly, it was apparent that Mexico wanted to find a way to back off without appearing to back down. Thus, when Sen. Adlai Stevenson III of Illinois introduced a bill that would have curtailed Export-Import Bank credits to Mexico if the natural gas agreement went through without the approval of Secretary of Energy Schlesinger (Carter had named him to the newly created post), the Mexicans protested. Stevenson withdrew his resolution, and the Mexicans got their Export-Import Bank credit. In December 1977 Díaz Serrano and the Mexican minister for foreign relations met in Washington with Schlesinger, who gave them advice on how to rewrite their proposal with the U.S. natural gas companies so as to satisfy U.S. regulatory agencies.

López, now pilloried in the press, felt humiliated and betrayed. He abruptly cancelled the agreement with the U.S. pipeline companies. The incident, blown out of proportion in both countries, was for the Mexican leader yet another manifestation of U.S. domination.[19]

chapter 6

THE SOCIAL CRISIS

In Mexico, it is often said, what matters more than what the United States *does* is what Mexican officials *believe* it has done. This sentiment is a variation on the ongoing Latin American complaint that the United States never does anything *for* a Latin American country that has no economic benefit for the giver. The United States has become understandably irritated by such attitudes, especially in Mexico's case, for no Latin American country, most Americans strongly believe, has benefitted so much from U.S. economic aid, both direct and indirect. American leaders repeatedly speak of a "special relationship" with Mexico yet perceive in their neighbor not gratitude but defiance. Public and private expressions of friendship and cooperation by Mexican and American leaders facilitate understanding and negotiation over common problems; mutual suspicion and political wrangling prevent their resolution.

Perhaps no U.S. president has suffered more from this political predicament in his dealings with Mexico than Jimmy Carter, who genuinely liked Mexicans, respected their culture, and treated his Mexican counterpart as an equal. He entered office with sincere convictions of Mexico's *cultural* importance to the United States (as has President George Bush, though in Bush's estimation, Mexico's *strategic* value is doubtless a more critical factor) and early in his administration directed his staff to give Mexican affairs a high priority. In August 1978 National Security Advisor Zbigniew Brzezinski authorized Presidential Review Memorandum No. 41, "Review of U.S. Policies toward Mexico." Its purpose was to prepare Carter for his visit to Mexico the following February by marshalling data and recommendations from 14 differ-

81

ent agencies in the federal bureaucracy that, in one way or another, have an interest in U.S. policy toward Mexico.

The chair of the interagency sessions was the redoubtable Viron "Pete" Vaky, assistant secretary of state for inter-American affairs, one of the most knowledgeable students of U.S. policy toward Latin America in or outside government. But the accumulated wisdom of these meetings did not produce what Carter expected. On the contrary, wrote Robert Pastor,

> It soon became apparent why it was so difficult for the United States to achieve a coherent, integrated policy toward Mexico. Routinely, from forty to eighty people attended the meetings, with seemingly nothing in common but that their decisions had some impact on Mexico. U.S. domestic agencies probably have as much and sometimes more influence on Mexico than the State Department, and none wants to permit either State or the White House to "interfere" with its policy. The essence of the President's administrative problem was to persuade the domestic agencies to be more responsive to his policies and priorities than to the agency's constituency in the country and in Congress.[1]

The Immigration and Naturalization Service (INS) was present to speak about immigration and the growing concerns over illegal entries from Mexico; the Department of Agriculture to manifest the position of U.S. farmers over Mexican agricultural imports; the Departments of the Treasury and Commerce, the International Trade Commission, and the special trade representative to voice respective opinions about U.S. trade policy with Mexico; the Treasury Department again to detail its concerns with Mexico's financial status; and the Defense Department to convey the military's views. Assembled with them in these meetings were advocates for urban and state governments and sundry independent regulatory agencies. Even the Department of Housing and Urban Development had a Mexican connection and thus earned a seat at the table.

In the end, the meetings probably did more harm than good. The papers submitted by the often wrangling agencies not only lacked helpful information but probably reinforced Carter's growing frustration over trying to bend the Washington bureaucracy to do his bidding. With so many agencies involved, of course, leaks were inevitable. The Mexicans, suspicious after the diplomatic commotion over the natural gas pipeline, became convinced there was a conspiracy. By the time the recommendations reached the National Security Council (NSC) staff, writes Pastor, there was agreement that "the United States has a central interest in a stable, prosperous, and humane Mexico." With that inspirational directive, the discussants moved on to specific issues—immigration, trade, energy, and so on—only to hear U.S. officials complain about Mexico's unwillingness to discuss such matters in any meaningful way.

Their task was to find a means to manage a relationship they acknowledged was unmanageable. There was no point in pressing the Mexicans on an issue if they would not budge. Nor was there any reason in belaboring new ideas the Mexicans were not interested in discussing. For want of anything better, they opted for "organizational gimmicks," such as the binational commission or "coordinator." On energy, for example, it was fruitless to persuade the Mexican government that American deliberations over Mexican oil production was anything more than a strategic calculation. Obviously, the United States, which had doubled its imports of Middle Eastern oil since 1975, looked to Mexican production as a welcome source and, of course, as a means of reducing Mexico's economic dependence. But it was also clear that the NSC staff was alert to the social consequences of Mexico's rapid economic development.[2]

Not surprisingly, this was similar to the judgment expressed by a group from the College of Mexico in their sessions with López Portillo and PEMEX director Jorge Díaz Serrano a year earlier. The Mexican president had largely ignored their advice. His decision to do so, however, was not so abruptly made as it may have appeared to U.S. observers. Accustomed to interpreting Mexican economic policy largely in the context of the U.S.–Mexican economic interdependence, U.S. observers may have been distracted from the sometimes bitter political battles *within* the Mexican government about the nation's exploitation of its newfound petroleum wealth. In the beginning of López's *sexenio* the Mexican government expressed its *intention* to avoid profligate spending of its petroleum wealth and did not wish to encourage consumer debt in purchase of durable goods or to subsidize food imports.

But the prospect of a quick jolt to the economy, to say nothing of the profiteering opportunities, was a persuasive argument for a gaggle of expansionists (particularly in PEMEX) in the ministerial battles that raged between 1978 and 1981. By the latter date, those who advocated a more cautionary policy, led by president-to-be Miguel de la Madrid, then serving as minister of programming and budgeting, finally won out. De la Madrid demanded (and got) the resignation of the voluble PEMEX czar Díaz Serrano. But by then it was too late. Díaz had already expanded oil production, borrowed money on future petroleum revenues, and enriched himself and his buddies. When de la Madrid became president in 1982, the Mexican government was practically bankrupt.[3]

These often internecine political battles were under way when Carter made his controversial visit to Mexico City in February 1979. It was a meeting of two proud leaders, each frustrated by growing public doubts in his country about the ability of either government to manage the political and economic forces at work in the U.S.–Mexican relationship. Carter brought with him no clear negotiating agenda save for the NSC staff recommendation that he ought to consult first with López before making any policy recommendations on the numerous issues the interagency bureaucrats had discussed in their fruitless efforts to provide the president with a "coherent, integrated" set of recommendations on U.S. policy toward Mexico. Some of the ablest and certainly most well-intentioned public servants had wrestled with a seemingly insurmountable and unresolvable problem in the U.S.–Mexican relationship: virtually every issue that offers the prospect of negotiability (i.e., trade or energy) also has an intangible feature related in one way or another to national sovereignty, dignity, or identity. Thus, few are susceptible to traditional means of diplomatic resolution. The notion of a "special relationship," Pastor has astutely observed, was of little help to Carter's advisors because it presupposed special concessions from Mexico in return. Washington could not deal with Mexico in the same way it negotiated with major European countries, they knew. A "sensitive" approach to Mexico appeared to be the only acceptable choice.[4]

Despite these impediments, the 1979 meeting accomplished a great deal. In what some regarded as a curious switch in role playing, López talked about the United States as global giant; Carter reaffirmed the U.S. commitment to the North–South dialogue and showed his understanding of the problems of developing nations. Later, in the much-publicized "battle of the toasts," López, as Mexicans are wont to do, expounded on the differences between the two nations and, the press reported, "lectured" the U.S. president about Washington's unfair treatment of a neighbor. Carter tried to mitigate his host with a bit of humor about "Montezuma's Revenge," then spoke eloquently about the bonds of neighborhood.

His frustrations vented, López warmed to his guest's sincerity and declared, "We see in you a leader who has sought to revive the moral foundations of the political institutions of the United States."[5] The following day they sat down and came to substantive agreement on a number of issues, including drug control and gas imports and resolved to discuss further another problem that was rapidly becoming a volatile political question in both countries— immigration.[6] López gave Carter a warm sendoff at the airport. Most Americans quickly forgot López's words of farewell, but they retained a lasting image of their president "humbled" in the city of the Aztecs.

Carter came back to Washington with renewed determination to blend morality, reason, and power in U.S. policy toward Mexico. He reminded cabinet officers of the need for policies sensitive to Mexico and seconded the appointment of special coordinator of Mexican affairs to convey this sentiment to the myriad domestic agencies whose decisions affected Mexico. Because the Mexicans had not bothered to hire a lobbyist to advance their position on trade or immigration before Congress or the media (and the regular Mexican ambassador was disinclined to play the role), the notion that a presidential appointee could perform that task seemed, at first glance, a superb ploy. But the Mexican reaction was one not of gratitude but puzzlement and heightened speculation about what the president *really* intended. Their suspicions apparently proved correct when the coordinator spent more time advancing the cause of U.S. business interests in Mexico than playing his intended role as interlocutor.

The U.S.–Mexican relationship now began to take on an unintended and, in some ways, unforeseen shape. Throughout the postwar years the leaders of both nations often expressed opposing and sometimes sharply diverging views on a variety of issues. They had argued about the bracero program, trade, and the role of U.S. multinational corporations in Mexico; in international forums they had sharply disagreed about the Cuban revolution. In each of these disputes and crises they had endured powerful domestic challenges to their positions. Yet in none of these had they permitted the severing of the economic ties, and in their often starkly different approaches to world affairs they retained a sometimes begrudging but always noticeable mutual respect. They may have disagreed about the nature of (or even the existence of) a "special relationship," but each retained a faith that they could somehow manage it.

But in 1979 both Jimmy Carter and José López Portillo began to weaken in their ability to harness the considerable authority each possessed to monitor and direct the course of U.S.–Mexican affairs. The visible signs of this deteriorating strength appeared in a series of political disputes. In spring 1979 Carter became more apprehensive about the Sandinista guerrilla war against the dictator of Nicaragua, Anastasio Somoza Debayle, and insinuated the U.S. government in the struggle in a manner that persuaded most Latin American governments, including Mexico, that his real intention was to get rid of Somoza but deny the Marxist Sandinistas the fruits of victory by setting up a pro-American government. It was a distortion of his motives but widely believed. Carter was annoyed with the Mexican reaction but did not confront López on the matter.

Then, in October, López Portillo committed what was for Carter an unpardonable act: the Mexican president broke his pledge to permit the Shah of Iran, who had fled that country earlier in the year, to enter Mexico after his medical treatment for cancer in the United States. Carter was furious. His first reaction was to retaliate, but he was immediately confronted with a more menacing challenge; the takeover of the U.S. embassy in Teheran by students and the beginning of his political nightmare. This incident, more than anything, perhaps explains why Mexico receives only passing reference in Carter's presidential memoirs. "I was outraged," Carter wrote. "The Mexicans had no diplomatic personnel in Iran, had moved all their people out of the country, and did not need Iranian oil. We'd had every assurance from them that the Shah would be welcome. They had given us no warning of their reversal; apparently the President of Mexico had simply changed his mind. It was a serious blow."[7]

For Carter it was yet another reminder of Mexico's apparent ingratitude and refusal to accommodate a U.S. leader who, unlike his predecessors, was genuinely trying to achieve a new understanding with Latin America. In 1977 Carter had opened a U.S. Interests section in Havana and followed it with the momentous Panama Canal treaties the following year. He had left Mexico City in February 1979 bearing the plaudits of his Mexican host as champion of social justice and human rights. Yet a few months later when Cuban leader Fidel Castro landed at Mexico City's airport, López greeted him as fellow revolutionary ("one of the personalities of the century") and, in a succession of public declarations, denounced the U.S. economic embargo against Cuba, called the U.S. Naval Station at Guantánamo Bay an imperial outpost, and rejected as false American statements that the Cubans were shipping arms to Sandinista guerrillas.[8]

These and other declarations appeared to confirm what American leaders privately denigrate as the instinctive anti-Americanism they believe is fundamental to Mexican foreign policy. True, López unabashedly advanced Mexico's claim as regional power in Latin America and promoted himself as the third world's advocate. But López's criticism of U.S. policy toward revolutionary movements in Central America reflected Mexican political assessments about Isthmian discord. The Mexicans largely subscribed to the view that the Sandinista, and later Salvadoran, revolutionaries were struggling against social and political injustice. In this context, then, U.S. political and especially military pressures merely delayed the inevitable triumph of a determined, organized, and popular revolutionary struggle.

This was, of course, the general sentiment of most Latin American leaders. What distinguished the Mexican interpretation of Isthmian revolution was its essentially *strategic* character. In this sense, it paralleled that of the administration of President Ronald Reagan in the early 1980s. As Reagan later argued, bringing down the Sandinistas and preventing a guerrilla triumph in El Salvador was necessary to forestall Central America's collapse to Marxism-Leninism, the spread of guerrilla struggle into southern Mexico, and the flight of refugees northward to the United States. Mexico accepted the domino theory but drew opposite conclusions. If the United States intervened in the Central American struggle, its presence would not only exacerbate the conflict but reinforce the determination of vested political interests to maintain their control. As Central America's militaries benefitted from increased U.S. aid, governments would become more repressive, especially in the countryside.

The Mexicans were indeed alert to the spillover of guerrilla war and the flight of refugees into southern Mexico, a region vital to the nation's economic future and with a more penetrable border than the 2,000-mile frontier with the United States. But the way to protect that southern flank, they reasoned, was through acknowledgment of the inevitability of revolutionary change in Central America. To identify with the U.S. position on Central America on the grounds that the Americans were shielding Mexico from Communist insurgency was not only stupid but fraught with domestic political dangers. Such a policy would deny Mexico a moderating role among Central America's revolutionary movements and, more important, rouse the nation's vocal leftists into more furious denunciations.

López played the role of benefactor of the Sandinistas with political grandstanding and with the determination to restore Mexico's rightful place in

Central America. Unlike the United States, Mexico had no private business interests or Isthmian political allies to defend from revolutionary takeovers. Thus, as López proudly declared, Mexico's assistance to the revolution against Washington's "lackey" Somoza served the nobler purpose of sustaining the inalienable right of Nicaragua's oppressed people to self-determination. Before his regime fell, Somoza ridiculed the last-minute efforts of the Carter administration to coax the OAS into sending an inter-American contingent as an obvious effort to prevent a Sandinista takeover. In the last drive against Somoza's government in July 1979, the Mexican president sent ammunition to the Nicaraguan southern front and, when Somoza abruptly fled the country, dispatched his presidential plane to San José, Costa Rica, in order to transport the newly formed junta north to Managua.

In early 1980 López visited Managua and was feted by the *comandantes*, still flushed with the pride of victors. Unlike the American government (then providing the bulk of aid to the fledgling Government of National Revolution), Mexico stood by its pledge of unconditional aid without the politically debilitating requirement that it be apportioned on terms set by the lender. The Mexican economic commitment was considerable: López agreed to facilitate Mexican–Nicaraguan cooperation in mining, construction, shipbuilding, oil, fishing, transportation, health, and education. Mexico provided equipment to build telephone and telegraph facilities, credit to purchase badly needed medical supplies, and monies to purchase Mexican buses. With a cooperative arrangement between the National Food Program of Nicaragua and the Mexican Food System, the two governments committed their efforts to securing regional food self-sufficiency. In the meantime, López pledged to feed the Nicaraguan people with rice and beans, Mexican staples. Already, Cuban technicians and professionals were entering Nicaragua, which reinforced Castro's boast of solidarity with the Sandinista revolution and Cuba's willingness to send its people to help. Mexico did not send Mexicans, but its commitment to Nicaragua in these early years of the revolution was vital.

In October 1979, when reformist officers in El Salvador brought down the military government, the Mexican PRI hosted in Oaxaca a gathering of nationalist, democratic political representatives—socialists and populists but not Christian Democrats or Communists because they fell under "foreign influence." A few months later, after the reformist government in San Salvador had fallen to a rightist coup, the Mexicans began courting the leaders of the Faribundo Martí National Liberation Front (FMLN) and warned the Americans about making Central America a battleground in the East–West conflict. In September 1980 Mexico joined France in a communiqué to the U.N. Security Council, calling for the recognition of the FMLN and its political wing, the Revolutionary Democratic Front, as the "representative political force" in El Salvador. This move represented the high tide of Mexico's political assertiveness in the region.[9]

There was no abrupt shift in Mexican foreign policy in Central America.

Indeed, when the Reagan administration singled out the Isthmus as an area of vital concern to the national interests of the United States and made it a flashpoint in the East–West conflict (and, not insignificantly, provided an off-Broadway stage for the anti-Communist theatrics of Republican conservatives, especially Sen. Jesse Helms of North Carolina), the Mexican government held fast to its earlier position that diplomatic negotiation among the Central American governments and dialogue between opposing political forces within each country, especially in El Salvador and Nicaragua, offered the best prospect for resolution of conflict. Mexico was an enthusiastic member of the four-nation (the others were Panama, Venezuela, and Colombia) Contadora group, which authored a significant peace initiative for Central America.

But there was a noticeable weakening in Mexico's presence in the region. Most American observers attributed this largely to the ominous economic downturns that began in 1980 and led to the collapse of the "new" Mexico that López had forecast early in his administration. These troubles culminated in the financial crisis of 1982, when oil revenues, which government forecasters had declared would produce $20 billion in revenue, yielded $15 billion. The $5 billion shortfall came just as Mexico's foreign debt hit $80 billion, more than half of it accumulated during López's *sexenio*. Numerous private businesses that had joined the government in the avid pursuit of loans, went bankrupt, and Mexicans sent $20 billion annually out of the country. Emulating Echeverría's populism, López dramatically proposed a series of emergency measures—peso devaluation, severe restrictions on dollar withdrawal, and, finally, nationalization of the banks. Even so, Mexico required a bailout from the U.S. government and the International Monetary Fund.[10]

The effect, undeniably, altered the economic (and in subtle ways the political) dynamic in the U.S.–Mexican relationship. As the economic grip tightened on the Mexican middle class, the political opposition became more combative and broadened its base, especially in the states along the U.S. frontier. Criticism of the government's policies and especially its continued economic presence in the private sector sharply escalated. Throughout the 1980s the condition of the Mexican economy was a central, often dominating, factor in the government's relations with the United States. During the annual Mexico–U.S. Interparliamentary Conference (a gathering of legislators from both countries, initiated in 1961), the discussions of common issues grew sharper and mutually recriminatory.

None produced such conflicting views as immigration. Ironically, the reconsideration of immigration policy and the "Mexican connection"—which precipitated a prolonged political debate in the United States that began in the early 1970s—became a debilitating feature in Carter's efforts to improve U.S. relations with Mexico. The president's secretary of labor, Ray Marshall, a University of Texas economist, had come to Washington with strong notions about the impact of alien workers—especially Mexicans, illegal and legal—

on employment opportunities for Americans. Unemployment in summer 1977 was 7.1 percent; for agricultural workers it reached 11.7 percent, although farm-worker labor leaders argued that it was much higher.

Organized labor, which had endorsed Carter for president, pushed for immigration reform as a means of dealing with not only the high unemployment rate of domestic farm workers but the condition of the workplace. Southwest agro-business wanted a return to some regularity in the migratory work force or perhaps a revival of the bracero program as a means of dealing with the uncertainties of using "illegals." Marshall wanted to reduce the supply and demand of alien labor, an approach consistent with that advocated by the AFL-CIO and the United Farmworker Organization headed by César Chávez. When Carter told the INS to enforce the law with greater vigor, he signalled that he had apparently come down on the side of the reformers, not the growers.

Had the agricultural worker program come under the scrutiny of one department, there might have been a resolution of this issue. As it was, not only did the Departments of Agriculture and Labor play an important (and often disputatious) role, but so did the Immigration Task Force of the Domestic Policy Staff and numerous southwestern representatives and senators. Carter, himself a former farm owner, expressed some sympathy for the problems of southwestern agro-business, especially in Texas, where he overruled Marshall in favor of growers in Presidio who wanted to bring in Mexican workers, using the shopworn argument that domestic farm workers were unavailable. (In a similar case involving Utah growers, the president held firm against importing alien workers.) In August 1977 Carter announced a sweeping proposal for immigration reform: enforcement of entry laws, an increase in the Border Patrol to curtail the migration of undocumented workers and fines for businesses employing those who eluded the Border Patrol, amnesty for undocumented aliens, and economic aid for sending countries, especially Mexico. Before his term ended in the ignominy of the Iran hostage crisis and a political shellacking from Ronald Reagan, Carter was disconsolately referring to immigration as more complex and equally as frustrating as the Strategic Arms Limitation Talks with the Soviet Union.[11]

In the United States there commenced a prolonged, occasionally vituperative, debate over immigration—its economic, political, and cultural legacy—that ultimately culminated in the Immigration Reform and Control law of 1986. Begun with a singular purpose of "regaining control over our borders," the discourse over immigration in the "decade of immigration" confronted American leaders again with the task of defining "what kind of nation we want to be." Such remarks represented the nobler, purposeful sentiments expressed in this debate. Its darker features, however, reflected latent American xenophobia about newcomers, especially those who had entered illegally, and legitimate concerns about the capability of social service agencies and educational systems—particularly in the heavily affected cities of Houston,

Chicago, and Los Angeles—to accommodate their needs. There were somber warnings about a vast, unassimilable, non-English-speaking American subculture. Similar cultural doomsday prophecies had appeared at the turn of the twentieth century, in the heyday of the great 40-year migration of southern and eastern Europeans that began in 1880.

Immigration was an old question in the U.S.–Mexican diplomatic agenda. What gave it an urgency in the 1980s was the inability of either government to isolate it from the more rancorous arena of cultural politics. Given the American political tradition of reconciling ethnic or regional issues through compromise, negotiation, and mutual benefits to the contesting parties, there was diminished interest (and increased risk) in tolerating Mexico's seeming unhelpfulness as this debate went on. When a U.S. leader told his Mexican counterpart that national sovereignty was at stake in controlling U.S. borders against illegal entry, the latter responded that bilateral problems cannot be solved through unilateral means. No Mexican leader, it was said, could deny a citizen the right to go north and look for work.

The movement in the United States to confront illegal immigration with more effective measures occurred almost simultaneously with another immigration crisis in southern Mexico. Its provenance originated in the furiosity of the Guatemalan government's counter-insurgency in the late 1970s against guerrilla movements in the countryside and its human rights violations, which severely tested López Portillo's efforts to improve relations with the two countries. Twice, the Mexican president postponed a goodwill visit to Guatemala. In May 1981, however, 13 Guatemalan peasants took over the Brazilian embassy in Guatemala City as a protest against the regime's counter-insurgency. They were later granted asylum in Mexico.

The Guatemalan military now launched yet another campaign in the highland provinces, killing hundreds of peasants and burning their villages. Many began fleeing across the virtually unguarded Mexican–Guatemalan border, where they established makeshift camps, waiting for an opportunity to return. By 1982 20,000 Guatemalans lived in camps in the Mexican province of Chiapas. Two years later the numbers had increased to 150,000. Mexico had long taken justifiable pride in its tradition of receiving political exiles and its leaders often posed as benefactors of the persecuted. But the wretched Guatemalans in Chiapas were a different matter. Employing a logic often used by Americans in debating immigration laws, Mexican officials concluded that publicizing the camps would result in even greater numbers crossing into Mexico from Guatemala.

In early 1981, with little publicity, the Mexicans began expelling the Indians. By summer, however, as expulsions continued, there were outcries from the Mexican public against the practice, and the government hastily established an interagency commission to coordinate refugee aid. The director of the agency pledged that in the interest of humanity and social justice there would be no further removals, as the president had promised, but the minister of interior was less sympathetic, declaring that the Guatemalans were taking land and jobs from unemployed Mexicans. The director of migratory affairs, Diana Torres Arcieniega, was more blunt. Immigration from Guatemala explained much of the "social disintegration, rise in population, poverty, promiscuity, ignorance, delinquency, violence, [and] anarchism" in contemporary Mexican society.[12]

Mexican officials initially sought to deal with the problem with increased vigilance on the southern frontier, maintenance of friendly relations with Guatemala, and continued adherence to Mexico's traditional position on refugees. But, as occurred in Washington during the thrashing out of a new immigration law to deal with undocumented aliens, there was an intragovernmental debate over policy. The Foreign Relations Secretary, not unexpectedly, adhered to the notion that Mexico's stance must conform with international moral standards, but the Interior Secretary had the assigned task of internal security and immigration control. Given the diminishing economic condition of the nation, the hardliners eventually won out. In 1982 Mexico was not only broke but had lost the ability to feed itself. Its lofty economic plan for the Caribbean Basin had collapsed before a more aggressive U.S. version (the Caribbean Basin Initiative), which benefitted Washington's allies in Central America and reinforced the counter-insurgency program of the Guatemalan government. Guatemala's military, in turn, now found kindred spirits among their Mexican counterparts who looked on immigration as a security issue. There was a tacit understanding that Mexico and Guatemala would not permit their sometimes conflictive public stances to frustrate efforts for a "pragmatic" relationship.

Such a delicate balancing act could not survive the increasing external pressures on both governments. In 1983, following criticism of Mexican refugee policies by the United Nations High Commission for Refugees, de la Madrid pledged to safeguard the rights of Guatemalans on Mexican soil. But the expulsions continued, and Mexican vigilance over the camps increased. Chiapas, the state in which most of the refugees were living, was historically a region of social and political strife. With its vulnerability to fleeing Guatemalan refugees and its strategic importance—80 percent of national oil production is in the South—it now became a central political concern for the Mexican government. As American criticism of Mexico's "insensitivity" to U.S. concerns over illegal entries on the northern border continued, the Mexican government was undertaking a large-scale (and, given the budgetary crunch, ambitious) economic and military strengthening of this region. Mexico tried to be more accommodating to Guatemalan (and U.S.) pressures to repatriate the refugees but refused to accept involuntary repatriation, which meant, in effect, turning over the Guatemalans to their persecutors. Encouraged by the U.S. government's opposition to the Contadora movement, the Guatemalan government became more aggressive in its dealings with Mexico. In January and April 1984 Guatemalan planes strafed the refugee camps at

Trinitaria and El Chupadero. The Mexican government then began moving the refugees into camps in the interior. When they refused to leave their communal villages near their homeland, the Mexican military forced them to leave, then burned their villages.

Mexico had reluctantly accommodated Guatemala's counter-insurgency campaign, one of the vilest and most inhumane in the Americas. Alert to Reagan's intention to militarize the Central American conflict, the Guatemalans skillfully played a diplomatic game. In August 1984, when the Nicaraguan government—to the apparent befuddlement of Washington—agreed to the Contadora peace initiative, Guatemala joined the Sandinistas in signing. It was a signal for Reagan to act. A few months later the U.S. government restored economic and military aid to Guatemala, denied since 1977 because of that country's human rights abuses.[13]

By then the U.S. Congress was embroiled in the battle over U.S. policy in Central America. What distracted it was the parallel issue of illegal immigration, an issue that had sprung to political life again in February 1981 with the publication of the report of the Select Commission on Immigration and Refugee Policy. One of its members was Sen. Alan Simpson, a Wyoming Republican, who undertook what appeared a hopeless cause—regaining control of U.S. borders. Unless it was confronted, he said, unchecked immigration imperilled the nation's cultural identity and institutions. An "illegal" could acquire a "green card" (which entitled him to work in the United States) and with that get a social security number, a union card, a food stamp identity card, a Medicare-Medicaid card, a driver's license, and so on. Few of Simpson's colleagues disputed his evidence; fewer still wanted to take the political risk of championing reform of the system. Hispanic groups, which had become more visible in the 1970s and, with the extension of the voting rights laws to the Southwest, more threatening politically, were bound to challenge him.

Yet Simpson took them on. In 1981, as Simpson's Republican colleagues shied away from a fight, he sought confrontation outside Washington and found grudging acceptance on Capitol Hill. The Reagan administration supported immigration reform and suggested seemingly new means of achieving it. Ultimately, however, the administration relied on earlier proposals—sanctions against employers, verification of workers, and amnesty—to effect a workable law. And once the bill was in the legislative hopper, the assault began—from Hispanics who feared prejudicial treatment of Hispanic-surnamed Americans, from immigration reform lobbies who wanted more funding, from immigration agents who derided it as ineffective, and, predictably, from growers who wanted a reliable work force. Not even Simpson liked what he saw in the bill and joined with Reps. Romano Mazzoli and Peter Rodino in fashioning a better one. For the next three years Congress wrangled. By 1984, as Reagan looked to reelection and a larger percentage of the Hispanic vote, the supporters of reform wearied. The League of United Latin American Citizens effectively lobbied against the bill, and when Democratic candidates, including presidential nominee Walter Mondale, began courting Hispanic voters, the bill was in trouble. On the House floor, Hispanic Americans (more sensitive to the plight of the undocumented) quarreled with Italo- and Irish-Americans (who spoke of the *legal* entry of their ancestors) about the fairness of U.S. immigration law. Occasionally, wrote Thomas Weyr, a normally dispassionate colleague would interject the most remembered comment of the debate: "We're losing control of our borders."[14]

In earlier debates about immigration reform, legislators had exhibited more confidence about how to compromise such diverse matters as labor needs, refugee concerns, and social justice into a workable law. But as the sometimes rancorous and disputatious legislative sessions went on, there were disturbing remarks about "uncontrollable borders" or the "future of the American way of life" interspersed with grim reminders that "something must be done." The United States had, unarguably, one of the fairest immigration policies in the history of the nation-state, yet it now stood victimized by its own generosity. Clearly, immigration laws must be enforced, labor needs must be met, and civil rights must be respected, they agreed, but, not surprisingly, they could not agree on the most effective means. More disturbingly, they were unsure about the effectiveness of any law they might pass. As Reagan stormed to victory in November, immigration reform appeared doomed.

Two years later, essentially the same bill became law. The reasons for this turnaround are many. For one thing, a liberal/conservative coalition made political compromise possible. Agricultural interests, especially in the Southwest, won a considerable economic concession when migratory farm labor received special consideration under the proposed law. Granted that, legislators who had previously stymied efforts to get a new law now joined forces with the reformers and persuaded the Hispanic holdouts that the bill before them offered a better alternative to a putatively harsher measure if Congress delayed. Amnesty (the process of legalizing the status of undocumented aliens continuously in the country from 1 January 1982), a critical feature of the new law, would be imperilled if nothing was done. Already some militant reformists, using INS estimates, were casually introducing unsettling statistics: 20 million "illegals" in the United States (a ridiculously exaggerated number) tremendous demands on social service facilities in heavily affected cities, and an alarming rise in prostitution, crime, gang activity, disease, and drugs. Several members of Congress, theretofore hesitant about changing immigration patterns that had proved economically practical for generations, trooped down to San Diego or El Paso and returned with horror stories about a "war zone" on the border.

The U.S.–Mexican border has always been a conflict zone, but until the early 1980s the United States had been able to manage the inevitable social problems associated with interdependent economies and the international labor force that served them. INS agents and the Border Patrol were accustomed to the irritations of policing a 2,000-mile border where there are 500,000 *legal* crossings every day. They did not have to hassle every person who crossed because there were always checkpoints inland where the Border Patrol could intercept "illegals." But economic factors fueled a border crisis in the 1980s.

In 1982 the severe downturn in the Mexican economy and the conflict in Central America added considerably higher numbers to the pool of regular commuters. Mexicans who had lost their jobs joined desperate Central Americans hovering on the border, waiting for a chance to cross. Many Americans tacitly accepted their absorption in the labor force because they were an integral part of the U.S. economy. The INS found proof of this through its well-publicized raids in 10 cities on businesses employing undocumented workers in 1982—"Operation Jobs."

During the discussions about the Simpson-Mazzoli bill, Congress had considered the proposed law's undeniably severe economic implications for Mexico and discussed a proposal alloting Mexico 50,000 slots in visas. Surprisingly, observed a Mexican commentator, there was less preoccupation with this suggestion than with stories about ill treatment of undocumented Mexican laborers in the United States that were brought to light during the INS sting operation. For most Mexicans, maintaining a supply of labor from Mexico to the United States was of such obvious economic importance to both countries that, inevitably, they believed, the gringos would come to their senses and live with that reality. The Mexican government did not question the United States' sovereign right to control admission of aliens to its soil, but considered attempts to stop the movement of an international labor force with a restrictive immigration law not only contradictory but unrealistic.[15]

The explanation for such an undertaking lay in the unanticipated social consequences of migrations *within* the United States *and* Mexico. As southwestern U.S. and Mexican agriculture were modernized in the 1940s, Mexican Americans and Mexicans were driven from the land. In the United States they were displaced by a more docile and thus more reliable Mexican work force. They migrated into the cities of the Southwest, where many of them, poorly educated and socially alienated, lost any sense of belonging to any community save that of the barrio. They lived in what Chicano historian Rudolfo Acuña has called "Occupied America." They did not share proportionately in the material blessings of American life or in its economic opportunities. In the 1970s labor economists (among them Vernon Briggs, Jr.) argued persuasively that the undocumented worker from Mexico was bypassing the agricultural marketplace in order to sell his labor to employers in the cities. The casualty in this battle for low-skilled jobs, said Briggs, was the Chicano.[16]

In Mexico, where the "Green Revolution" commenced during World War II, the small farm owner ultimately lost out as the Mexican agricultural economy was modernized. In the Bajío, the "breadbasket" of central Mexico in Guanajuato and Michoacán, government policies favored farmers with irrigated land, who began contracting with U.S. multinational corporations to grow sorghum, wheat, and vegetables for American markets. Farmers with poorer or unirrigated land and unable to use the agricultural technology available to larger producers failed to benefit. They found it increasingly difficult to sustain their families with decreasing yields of traditional crops of beans and corn, staples of the campesino diet, and became part of the migratory cycle to large farms in Sinaloa and Sonora and the United States. In many of the rural villages of central Mexico, the prospect of seasonal employment for male family members in the United States became critical for the well-being of entire families.[17]

Both Mexico and the United States adjusted to these migrations. Whatever the social cost, it was argued, the benefits of economic modernization would be great enough to compensate for the displacement of rural peoples. Americans took as faith that agricultural policy should benefit the urban consumer, which meant that agricultural producers had to lower labor costs in order to keep prices low. The Mexican government was ambiguous: it gave the campesino land but not liberty, and its economic modernization program intentionally favored the agro-export food producer. Those tossed off the land could be absorbed into the urban marginal work force or become migrant laborers. And, in both countries, there were social programs designed to provide an underpinning for those left behind.

The rural social scar in both countries was largely hidden from the sight of the urban middle class until desperate rural migrants began showing up in ever larger numbers in Mexico City and straining its already overburdened social services. Ultimately, it was believed, these newcomers would adapt and join the marginal labor force. But there was a disturbing parallel dynamic at work: more and more of the newcomers were indigenous people pushed off their land in Oaxaca or out of their villages in Tabasco by the government's relentless drive to develop southern Mexico. Some, such as the Mixtecs of Oaxaca, a severely underdeveloped state, bypassed the capital altogether and headed for the border, principally Tijuana, where they resisted assimilation into the traditional mestizo culture by re-creating their own *colonies*. Ultimately, they marked out a special place for their families in the border economies.[18]

The predominate economic philosophy on both sides of the border holds that modernization, despite its social costs, is ultimately beneficial for both society and the individual. Dynamic economies generate opportunities for all. Some benefit more than others, but all should benefit. Through economic and social policies, the state manages economic development and cushions the shock of the process. But in the early 1980s, as Americans were distracted by the numbers of illegal entries or the random violence, those who measure the social barometer of the border were alerted to something else. Socialists called it the "immiseration" or "proletarianization" of a labor force; anthropologists described it as a border "cultural enclave"; geographers measured the human demand on a region of limited resources; and economists (and a few novelists) characterized it as the frontier between a first world and third world country or the encounter between a postindustrial and developing economy.

A proper metaphor for what two governments and two economies and two cultures had bequeathed is two "hourglass societies." A generation ago, the proper geometrical metaphor for the United States was a diamond, and for Mexico a pyramid. As *numerical* representations—a large middle class in the diamond-shaped society, a large lower class in the pyramid-shaped society—those designations yet hold true. But the proper geometrical metaphor for the middle class of *both* societies is the hourglass, for it conveys the common middle-class fear about a diminishing standard of living, *regardless of the size of the middle class or economic opportunities.*

TWO NATIONS, ONE FUTURE

The adjustment of the "safety valve" on the northern frontier was but one of several Mexican concerns in 1986. Earlier in the year, in a series of highly publicized and controversial hearings before the Western Hemisphere Affairs Subcommittee of the Senate Foreign Relations Committee, Sen. Jesse Helms, a North Carolina Republican and one of the harshest critics of the Mexican "bailout" four years before, subjected Mexico to a tongue lashing. After perfunctory compliments for Mexico's achievements—"a political stability unmatched in Latin America"—he cataloged American concerns:

We are disturbed because we see a condition of flight from Mexico. We see a flight of capital. We see a flight of workers. We see a flight of drugs. . . . We know that a lack of funding is not the problem. We know that billions of dollars have fled from Mexico in the last 3 years. We see Mexican citizens making astonishing large investments in United States real estate and other ventures. We see large houses and expensive automobiles being purchased here, and large bank deposits, both here and in Switzerland. . . . We need to know whether the massive nationalizations of banks and private industry have anything to do with the lack of investor confidence. We need to know whether massive state intervention in the economy has anything to do with Mexico's poor productivity. We need to know whether Mexico has official policies that discourage foreign investment. We need to know these things because one way or another, the United States taxpayer will shortly be asked to prop up the Mexican economy.

Mexico . . . is in a spiral downward. . . . When we see the flight of workers across our borders, poor people driven by desperation and hope, to seek jobs illegally in the United States, we know that Mexico is not doing its part for its own people. Mexico's socialized economy is exploiting the Mexican people. Should that economy collapse entirely, either of its own inefficiency or under pressure from Marxist guerrillas, the flood of refugees into the United States would become intolerable and human misery unbounded. When we see the flight of drugs, we know not only the degradation which this commerce spreads in our own country, but also the corruption which always accompanies this breakdown in the social order in the producing countries.

Apparently the senator was less concerned with the diplomatic repercussions of the hearings than his faith in the U.S. tradition of "free inquiry." Going to the "source," a word commonly used to distract public attention to the ominous escalation of drug consumption in the 1980s, required getting at the "root of the problems [which is] the failure of the democratic system in Mexico. Has the long-term political stability of Mexico been purchased at the price of political freedom? Has the dominance of one party for so long resulted in the breakdown of the checks and balances which any political system must have if it is to counteract corruption, inefficiency, and despotism?"[1]

The passage merits quotation, not for its putative accuracy—Helms's views about U.S. foreign policy, especially in Central America and Mexico, were manifestly reductionist in their telling—but as a succinct expression of opinions widely held by Americans and, with some important qualifications, by middle-class Mexicans as well. Even those academic specialists who were irritated with Helms for "Mexcio bashing" perceived in the hearings an opportunity to alert the U.S. public to issues in U.S.–Mexican relations that must be promptly addressed.

Denouncing Mexico for the rise in illegal immigration or undeniably higher trafficking in narcotics, wrote historian Alfred Stepan, was "no help at all." Nor was the emergency $5 billion loan hastily negotiated in June 1986 to forestall yet another crisis sufficient for Mexico's needs. Given that Mexico's political stability was crucial to U.S. national security, the United States, Stepan observed, had been fortunate. Since the economic collapse of 1982, he wrote, Mexico had experienced zero economic growth, the minimum wage had been halved, the standard of living for the middle class had sharply deteriorated, and oil revenues (which generated 50 percent of government revenues and 75 percent of Mexico's foreign exchange) had dropped by $6 billion—yet its political system had held firm. Mexico's government may have suffered diminished credibility with many Mexicans, especially in the Federal District of Mexico City and in the northern states, but it had not lost legitimacy. "The United States is not insulated . . . and Mexico's long-term stability has been an extremely important part of this."[2]

Why, then, Washington's dramatic burst of "Mexico bashing" in 1986? The immediate reason was the perceived (and probably justifiable) evidence that Mexican officials, once lauded by the Reagan administration for their cooperativeness in the U.S. campaign against narcotics, had become protectors and, in some cases, accomplices of drug traffickers. Testifying before the Helms committee, Donald Westrate of the Drug Enforcement Administration (DEA) and William von Raab of the U.S. Customs Service confirmed Justice Department allegations that narcotics smugglers had shifted operations from the southwestern United States to Mexico.

By 1985 Mexico had become the principal source of heroin and marijuana for American consumers and a major cocaine transshipment center. When U.S. officials pressed their Mexican counterparts to assist by shutting down stash houses on both sides of the border or by permitting air surveillance (with Mexican officers accompanying them), they were rebuffed. As von Raab explained, "As long as drug smugglers are free either to return their planes to Mexico and land in a safe haven or . . . penny ante drug smugglers are free just to quickly rush across the Rio Grande River and find themselves their own safe haven, the United States effort is doomed to failure. . . . At the heart of this [problem], in my personal opinion, is just the ingrained corruption in the Mexican law enforcement establishment. I believe that . . . with all the good intentions of the highest level officials in Mexico, until the corruption at the lower levels of law enforcement are corrected, we are never going to be able to solve this problem."[3] Some agents within the DEA would have reversed von Raab's order of official culpability: it was the corruption at the *highest* levels of the Mexican government that was at the "heart" of the problem.[4]

It is not all that difficult to understand why others in the Reagan administration—people ordinarily more circumspect in their public assessments about conditions in a strategic neighboring country—should join Helms in his denunciation of Mexico. From the beginning of World War II until the late 1970s, Mexico occupied a special, albeit subservient, place in the shadow of U.S. economic and military power. Mexico had deviated from U.S. strategic priorities in Latin America and resisted American entreaties to invoke "economic liberalism" by dismantling its state-operated business entities. Suffused with pride over its oil wealth and inundated with easy foreign loans, Mexico became defiant and tried to break the American grip.

Almost simultaneously Carter tried to inject legitimate American concerns about Mexico's choices and was rebuffed. Reagan followed with new overtures—among them the suggestion of a North American free trade union of Mexico, the United States, and Canada—and the creation of a Binational Commission and Joint Commission on Commerce and Trade. But neither these nor other regional structures were sufficient to fashion a new understanding with Mexico. The economic collapse of 1982 and the enforced austerity that followed persuaded Washington that Mexico would again become so dependent on U.S. goodwill and largesse that its government would have to accommodate American strictures. By mid-1985 the Mexicans had stopped the flow of oil to Nicaragua and reduced the number of state-run agencies, and President de la Madrid had trimmed the bloated Mexican governmental bureaucracy. Yet in 1986 Mexico was again the unaccommodating neighbor. It was "flooding" the United States with drugs and people. Its officials were uncooperative. Mexican defiance resurfaced. But this time it was for Washington an irrational defiance born not of oil wealth but of the Mexican government's refusal to admit that its economic policies had failed and its adamant defense of the political system. There appeared little short of desperate measures that the United States could do about this defiance save for allowing its harried officials to vent their rage.

A relationship crafted and directed by governments had not only expanded and become more complicated but had grown beyond the governments' capacity to manage. The "Mexican miracle" had come about because of the U.S. economic connection, but in the 1980s the U.S. economy, once the driving force in the global economy, appeared driven by forces in the global economy. Whatever economic leverage the United States retained in the relationship (when the Mexican government required emergency bailout loans in 1982 and 1986, Washington's role in arranging them was crucial) diminished if Mexico chose not to accommodate U.S. strictures. Mexico rejected the more radical solution of default (which Fidel Castro proposed), but as de la Madrid declared in a major television address to the Mexican people, Mexico retained a right to alter or annul arrangements with its creditors. As a prominent Mexican official stated, any settlement with the nation's creditors must incorporate terms that are "reasonable, equitable, and appropriate to the circumstances we are living—not what we have to pay but what we can pay—without further depressing the living standards of the Mexican people."[5]

In the course of the decade, as its government strained under a $100 billion debt, Mexico became the champion of debtors' rights among hemispheric governments. Although the Reagan administration disapproved of this course and publicly lectured Mexican officials on the folly of their economic policies, it quietly acquiesced in the face of geopolitical realities and resisted the entreaties of private lenders to "get tougher" with the Mexicans on the debt question. Seemingly unrelated factors intruded. Mexico could not pay off its debt and purchase American commodities at the same time. The farm belt and the Southwest, for example, were particularly susceptible to fluctuations in U.S.–Mexican commerce. In 1986 Washington lacked the political leverage it had in 1982 because of budgetary restraints imposed by the Gramm-Rudman-Hollings deficit reduction law and the demands of domestic social programs. Reluctantly the Reagan administration chose to "delink" the U.S. government from the uncertainties of another aid package to an economically troubled neighbor and turned its attention to "damage control" within the U.S. financial system. Mexico, thus freed from its role as "special debtor," became leader of the Cartagena Group of 11 Latin American governments, which resolved to reduce interest rates on their debts to below market rates.[6]

It was a Pyrrhic victory, but Mexico's maneuvering in the international debt adjustment that preoccupied lenders during the decade demonstrated political strength and determination. Although de la Madrid's economic reforms had fallen short of satisfying the most vocal American critics—they did not include the recommended privatization of "losing" state-run companies, for example—Mexico's economic strength remained impressive. A 1988 staff assessment prepared for the Joint Economic Committee of Congress declared, "Even if the United States and Mexico did not share a common border, Mexico's economic weight would be sufficient in its own right to command priority attention from Washington."[7] Even so, Mexico had experienced little growth during the 1980s, which meant that the government's economic reforms were imperilled by the need to absorb a labor force that had grown by 8 million new workers since 1980, which required a *minimum* growth rate of 4 percent; to restore purchasing power to its middle class; and to reduce pervasive social inequities.[8]

The PRI created the modern Mexican state, all the while using its rhetoric to position itself as protector of the powerless. In truth the powerless were the losers in the making of postrevolutionary Mexico. Yet however few economic and social benefits trickled down to *los de abajo,* however miserable the cities' squatter *colonias,* howere many landless or rootless rural migrants, those who clung to power in the decade of *la crisis* did not fear revolution from below.

Americans viewing the political turbulence in Mexico in the 1980s, much of it in the border states, correctly identified the economic crisis as the spark for the resurgence of the opposition party, PAN, but misinterpreted what it portended for Mexico's political future. They compounded this error with smug reassurances that U.S. pressures for economic liberalism and American condemnations of undeniable fraud in Mexican state elections in 1986, particularly in Chihuahua, largely explained the Mexican government's feeble gestures toward American-style democracy. American arrogance toward Mexico has diminished considerably since the era when Woodrow Wilson spoke of "teaching them to elect good men," but it retains a hold on the American consciousness, however muted.

Wilson refused to deal with a Mexican government he regarded as illegitimate; Reagan put that government on probation. American authorities not only questioned Mexico's economic policy but also its domestic political agenda. The former was perhaps excusable, given the inseparable links between the U.S. and Mexican economies. Mexico yielded to American pressures for economic austerity and retracted its commitments to Central American revolutionaries. Its political resolve apparently weakened by the rising chorus of middle- and upper-middle-class criticism, the ruling PRI appeared vulnerable in the electoral arena. In the general discrediting of the populism associated with Echeverría and López's nationalization of the banks, the PAN was thus thrust into the center of the political storm.

This was a role the PAN's leaders relished, especially because Washington in the Reagan era (a PAN delegation showed up at the 1984 Republican convention in Dallas) was receptive to their philosophy: economic opportunity, sanctity of private property, more autonomy to municipal governments, and the ridding of Mexican politics of a state-dominated party. The PAN's most persuasive argument was that the PRI would perhaps yield to the opposition in municipal politics but *never* give up a governorship or the presidency. In the 1986 elections in Sonora, Nuevo León, San Luis Potosí, Baja California, Chihuahua, Durango, and Sinaloa the PAN made impressive showings among business and religious groups, and in Chihuahua, among the urban poor as well, but failed to capture a state governorship until 1989, when it won in Baja California. Electoral fraud in Chihuahua, especially, received considerable press coverage in the United States.[9]

Given the character of U.S. politics, it is understandable why American leaders have come to believe that Mexico will never be run properly until the PRI willingly concedes power and that it is in the best interests of the U.S. government to apply economic and political pressure to achieve this. The problem with this approach is that it exaggerates the potency of the American connection, underestimates the resilience of Mexican leaders, and, most important, presumes that the PAN, which is doubtless well enough organized to win an election (if provided an honest ballot), has a program to confront Mexico's pressing economic and social problems. The PAN is not the Mexican version of the GOP. Its base has widened considerably since the 1950s, but it is still largely pro-business and Roman Catholic. However diminished the PRI's credibility was in the decade of *la crisis,* the PAN is not yet ready to supplant it.

Americans still believe that because the United States has played a critical role in Mexico's debt crisis, it is in a unique position to influence the manner and character of economic modernization and democratization. But they are too much distracted by the electoral battles—in Mexico's northern states and most recently in the presidential election of 1988, when the PRI candidate, Carlos Salinas de Gortari, confronted a serious threat from the Left in Cuauhtémoc Cárdenas (Lázaro's son)—and too inattentive to the struggle going on within the PRI and the government for control of their respective bureaucracies. Among the latter, indisputably, are public officials whose political and economic philosophies are synonymous with American thinking on what should be done in Mexico, but they risk much if identified as too pro-American.[10]

Their dilemma is more complicated than most Americans realize and only partly related to an instinctive resentment among Mexican officials of advice from foreign creditors, who argue that Mexico must restructure and modernize its economy or confront pauperism. Many Mexican economists acknowledge that the economy must be modernized but respond that there is no quick fix. A highly protected economy has wrought an enormous burden in inefficient and technologically backward state-run firms. Selling them to the private sector, as the U.S. government wishes, will not help very much in a debt-ridden and stagnant economy. The most inefficient cannot be sold and thus must be closed, which means hefty severance pay for displaced workers and state inheritance of even more debts. Furthermore, reducing subsidies on consumer goods and services, which even Mexicans admit must be done, entails tremendous risk. There are social benefits to these subsidies at every level of Mexican society. Removing them in the name of economic efficiency raises the cost of living, the number of unemployed, and, most important, the prospect of social turmoil.[11]

"Mexico and the United States," writes former Arizona Governor Bruce Babbitt, "are united by geography and divided by history." His is a fairly common interpretation of the U.S.–Mexican experience among those who have labored to understand how neighboring countries so often disagree about issues they should be able to resolve or how peoples misperceive one another so often that they cannot achieve mutual understanding. Once barren and unpopulated lands along a 2,000-mile border are now inhabited by 10 million Mexicans and Americans who watch as their respective governments (and local and state authorities on both sides of the border) wrangle over myriad issues that they must but cannot resolve. "The challenge for both our countries," Babbitt continues, "is to work together toward a coherent, generally understood and accepted set of bilateral policies grounded in a realistic understanding of the possibilities—and limitations—imposed by historical and cultural realities."[12]

In actuality, Mexico and the United States were once divided by geography and in modern times have been united by history. Neither government will admit it, but they have chosen this course. What divided them in the nineteenth century was the physical expanse of a desert, a region that remained a sparsely inhabited frontier for both countries until about World War II. Even today vast stretches of the U.S.–Mexican border are as desolate as the frontier of a century ago. Throughout the twentieth century, this frontier has been a zone of conflict and cooperation, of strife and amity, of tragedy and hope, of opportunity and despair. Almost 150 years of economic development has produced a border often characterized as the encounter between the first and third worlds, a postindustrial consumer society abutting a model of the new industrial economic order and its army of laborers. Its economic face is dotted with 1,800 *maquiladoras* employing 500,000 Mexicans, its environmental features are scarred by pollution, and its limited resources are strained by the demands of 10 million people.[13]

In the past, the dynamics of Mexican and American economic development has largely determined these countries' common political agenda, the complexity of which has explained both governments' frustration with trying to resolve the disputes that economic bonds have wrought. In this respect, the border they have commonly developed with their capital and labor represents their common triumph and their common burden. The social problems it has produced may not have been their intention but certainly represents their choices.

Since World War II, it was often said, "when the United States sneezes, Mexico catches cold." In the 1980s Mexico's economic collapse reverberated northward, resulting in diminished earnings for U.S. businesses tied to Mexican markets, losses of jobs in American plants, financial pressures on U.S. banks, and a recession in the border economy. By the end of the decade, some of the economic damage had been repaired: Mexico finally joined the General Agreement on Tariffs and Trade; the economies on both sides of the border had recovered, at least partially, their earlier vigor; and in early 1990 Mexico successfully negotiated a new debt agreement.[14]

Both countries entered the 1990s as debtors in a global economy that is not only more competitive but no longer governed by the U.S. economy. In the United States such vulnerability has sparked cries of "unfair trade practices"; in Mexico it has revived denunciations of U.S. penetration. But neither country can afford to retreat into protectionism. There is considerable optimism in the economic sphere as both countries apply the new technologies—in materials, production techniques, and organization of a labor force—to the industrial workplace. With materials substitution (advanced ceramics or fiber optics, for example) multinational companies are replacing metal parts in automobile engines and are vastly improving communication. Biotechnology offers Mexico what the "Green Revolution" failed to achieve: a revolution in agricultural production that will enable Mexico not only to export food but also to feed itself. Automation and robotization, dependent on computers for design and manufacturing, promise advances in quality and reduction of labor costs. Advanced technology has yielded a communications and information revolution, permitting greater strides in research and development, decentralization of production, and achievement of economies of scale. The implications for the social organization of the workplace (especially along the border) are profound: changes in management philosophy, sharing of skills, and more cooperation between those involved in the production process.[15]

Mexico and the United States confront something more uncertain than the most effective application of new technology to the interdependent economies they have created. In the 1990s each must deal with powerful social forces pressing from below. The metaphors once employed to differentiate them—the United States' diamond-shaped society with a large and vigorous middle class as opposed to Mexico's pyramidal social structure—have been supplanted by dual hourglass-shaped societies. In the hourglass society the greatest uncertainties—of a more abundant and rewarding life, of the prospects for advancement, and of a better future for one's children—exist among the middle class. Though these uncertainties are more visible and certainly more numerous in the United States than in Mexico, middle-class Americans now share a "fear of falling." Unlike the privileged who have "privatized" their lives—private schools for their children, privately funded health care, and, in some instances, their own security systems—the middle classes of both countries sense they are losing ground. For them, the fundamental question is no longer the just demand of social justice for those below them but the cost of providing it or, more ominously, the somber realization that a dynamic economy has been unable to rid either country of a permanent underclass. Mexico's underclass is proportionately much larger and its standard of living much lower, of course, but its unsettling presence is a troublesome social reality for both countries.[16]

The seriousness of this social crisis is undeniable, certainly for Mexico, but neither its political nor economic legacy can be precisely measured. There are both disturbing and reassuring signals on the Mexican horizon. Two years after Senator Helms's denunciation of endemic fraud in Mexican elections, when Salinas won a highly disputed presidential election, both Cuauhtémoc Cárdenas (representing the leftist coalition, the National Democratic Front) and Manuel Clothier (candidate of the PAN) denounced the outcome and, respectively, claimed victory. On 14 September 1988, following the announcement of the Electoral Committee of the Chamber of Deputies that Salinas was the president-elect, Cárdenas spoke to a throng in the spacious plaza of the Zócalo and called on Salinas to resign. Failure to do so, he said, meant that the people were compelled to choose between "indignity or violent confrontation." Clouthier, more subdued in his public statements and eschewing confrontation, asked his supporters to practice "civil disobedience" and "social, political, and economic non-cooperation." The Committee for Improved U.S.–Mexican Relations denounced Cárdenas as a socialist and "ruthless demagogue" who was inciting civil war in Mexico: "The United States cannot afford a civil war in Mexico by means of a Communist insurrection. A Soviet-dominated Mexico will force the United States government to mobilize the necessary troops to defend over 2,000 miles of border and to redeploy personnel from other continents. Several million people could die and the political refugees' invasion wouldn't be less than 15 to 20 million."[17]

Salinas was safely inaugurated in December 1988 and commenced with an economic program that incorporated austerity, structural reforms, and privatization, carried out in a political atmosphere of liberalization and greater tolerance for dissent. Before long, soothsayers in Washington were comparing the Mexican leader to the largely mythical creature they have fashioned in their political imaginations when pondering what kind of president Mexico should have. For Americans, the model Mexican leader is, fundamentally, a mestizo prototype of the U.S. president. The reality for any Mexican president, however, is sharply different. A more appropriate comparison, wrote the distinguished political scientist Wayne Cornelius, is the authoritarian leader of Eastern Europe, the Soviet Union, or China, who decides to reform the system from above and finds himself pushed by forces from below.[18]

In Mexico there is electoral legitimacy and revolutionary legitimacy. Americans tend to focus on the first, but for Mexicans the second can be of equal if not greater importance, particularly when they consider the revolutionary promise and the role of the state not only as intervenor but as benefactor and arbiter of social conflict. Those who argue that Mexico's leaders should confront economic reality and adjust to the modern global economy casually ignore the revolutionary legacy. The accelerating changes in the international economy have been accompanied by a general weakening of the state's commitment to welfare programs and minimum standards in income, medical services, education, housing, and nutrition. Argentina, Brazil, and Chile weakened before these international economic pressures in the 1970s. Mexico resisted simply because of the late-1970s petroleum boom, which allowed the government to fund its social programs, and, when the petrodollar well ran dry, because its leaders were able to invoke the myth of revolutionary legitimacy and the "social pact" of the PRI.[19]

Viewing Mexico's economic dilemmas and the political strife of recent years, some American observers are persuaded that the PRI should yield to reality and share power with a rival party, most likely the PAN, certainly in the presidency but perhaps also in control of the legislature. Mexico would then better adapt to international economic realities—free trade with the United States, for example—because its political rhythms would be more harmonious. The problem with this scenario is that it ignores the political reality that is modern Mexico—three, not two, great political divisions: the PRI, PAN, and PRD, the Partido de Revolución Democrática, founded in 1989 in a union of the Cardenistas and the socialist Left. Confronting the PRD, Salinas cut a deal whereby the PRI conceded more political clout to the PAN but not to the PRD. His maneuvering, coupled with highly publicized statements about closer economic ties with the United States, inspired laudatory comments from American leaders. Mexicans were at last free to determine their own economic future. What they failed to perceive was that liberalization in Mexico was deepening, not healing, the divisions in the country, that democracy challenged not only a statist party's power but also its claim as the benefactor and arbiter of social conflict, or that such a party's president could not proclaim himself as the champion of political reform and at the same time repress the democratic aspirations of a people. Sooner or later, whatever the 1990s promise for the economy of Mexico, the nation will have to deal with its glaring social inequities. Strengthening the bilateral economic ties between Mexico and the United States would inevitably incorporate such issues into the political relationship.[20]

To the north, among generally accusatory American observers of the Mexican condition, a parallel though less debilitating social process is under way. Its resolution may be properly reserved for the sovereign government of each country, though neither can afford to ignore the political and social implications of the economic matrices they have created. Most important, neither Washington nor Mexico City can deny the human links fashioned between two disparate cultures and peoples. Americans and Mexicans can find the common ground where the "special relationship" between neighboring countries must take root if it is to be less conflictual than in the past. They can do so by recognizing the unappreciated bonds between them. History has united them. One-third of the United States was carved from one half of Mexico. The Anglos not the Mexicans are the newcomers to the U.S. Southwest. More than any *nation* save Great Britain, Mexico occupies a special place in America's heritage. There are familial links between their peoples, fashioned by a migration that has not yet run its course. Seventy-five percent of the 20 million Hispanics in the United States are of Mexican heritage. More than most Americans, they feel a special bond with Mexico. Many call themselves "Mexicans" yet they are no less "American" than their compatriots. As do many Mexicans who criticize the United States' government but admire its culture and people, Americans of Mexican descent do not judge their ancestral country and its people by the character or policies of its government. They respect Mexico.

They represent the most durable Mexican connection, the unbreakable bond between two peoples and two nations with one future.

CHRONOLOGY

1810	Mexican war of independence begins.
1821	Mexico wins independence from Spain.
1835–1836	Texas rebellion.
1845	Texas annexed as U.S. state.
1846–1848	Mexican–American War.
1857	Mexican Constitution incorporates reforms limiting church property and military privileges.
1858–1860	Civil war between Conservatives/clerics and Liberals.
1861	Liberal victory; Benito Juárez becomes president; Mexico's moratorium on foreign debt leads to landing of British, French, and Spanish troops.
1862	Britain and Spain withdraw toops, but French drive inland and are defeated 5 May at Puebla.
1863	French troops drive Juárez from the Mexican capital.
1864	France installs Maximilian as emperor of Mexico.
1867	Maximilian executed; Juárez becomes president.

1872   Juárez dies.

1876   Porfirio Díaz leads no-reelection rebellion, begins 34-year
                rule (except for 1880–84). Extensive U.S. economic
                penetration of Mexico, especially in railroads and mining.

1910   Francisco Madero rebellion.

1911   Madero elected president; Emiliano Zapata demands agrarian
                reforms.

1912   Pascual Orozco rebellion in the North.

1913   Ten Tragic Days, 8–18 February. Madero and Vice President
                Jesús Maria Pino Suárez arrested and killed on orders of Gen.
                Victoriano Huerta. U.S. Ambassador Henry Lane Wilson, a
                critic of Madero, is indirectly implicated. President
                Woodrow Wilson refuses to recognize Huerta's government
                and brings economic and diplomatic pressure on Huerta.

1914   U.S. naval forces seize Veracruz in April; the city is occupied
                by the United States until November. Huerta forced into
                exile in the summer (dies two years later in an El Paso jail).
                Revolutionary struggle for power begins between the forces
                of Venustiano Carranza (Constitutionalists), Zapata, and
                Pancho Villa. World War I begins in Europe in August.

1915   Villa defeated at Celaya; United States gives de facto
                recognition of Carranza as Mexico's president. Plan of San
                Diego, calling on Mexicans in the U.S. Southwest to rebel
                and seize land, frightens many Americans.

1916   Villa raid on Columbus, New Mexico, prompts U.S.
                intervention under Brig. Gen. John J. Pershing. Wilson
                presents his unsuccessful Pan American Pact.

1917   Mexican Constitution is promulgated, with Article 27
                declaring subsoil properties the possession of the Mexican
                people; this sparks conflict with U.S. petroleum companies.
                United States enters World War I in April.

1919   Zapata killed.

1920   Carranza regime toppled; he flees Mexico City and is killed.
                Alvaro Obregón becomes president.

1923	After negotiations, U.S. government recognizes Obregón. Villa killed.
1923–1924	Civil War between discontented revolutionary generals.
1924	Plutarco Elías Calles becomes president.
1926	Calles's anticlerical measures incite revolts.
1927	Ambassador Dwight Morrow is sent to Mexico to negotiate petroleum disputes; he also helps in mediation of church–state conflicts.
1928	Obregón elected but assassinated. Calles begins six-year reign as *jefe politico,* selecting functionary presidents, the first of whom is Emilio Portes Gil.
1929	Official party—Partido Nacional Revolucionario (PNR)—founded. Pascual Ortiz Rubio elected president.
1930	United States begins to deport Mexican workers.
1932	Ortiz Rubio opposes Calles and is forced to resign; Abelardo Rodríguez named interim president.
1934	Lázaro Cárdenas becomes president, sends Calles into exile and revives agrarian reform.
1938	Cárdenas nationalizes petroleum; confrontation with the United States.
1939–1942	Sinarquista rebellion in rural Mexico; Partido Acción Nacional founded.
1940	Manuel Avila Camacho becomes president, promotes closer ties with United States.
1941	United States enters World War II in December.
1942	Bracero agreement with United States; Mexico enters World War II 30 May.
1945	Inter-American Conference on Problems of War and Peace at Chapúltepec.
1946	Miguel Alemán becomes president; Mexican industrialization intensifies; the PRN evolves into the new

official ruling party, Partido Revolucionario Institucional (PRI).

1947   Harry Truman visits Mexico; Alemán tours Washington, D.C., New York, and Kansas City.

1952   Adolfo Ruiz Cortines becomes president.

1954   United States institutes "Operation Wetback," the massive deportation of uncontracted Mexican workers from the United States.

1958–1964   Adolfo López Mateos's *sexenio;* U.S. economic penetration of Mexico increases.

1964   Bracero program ends; Chamizal strip at El Paso/Ciudad Juárez returned to Mexico; Gustavo Díaz Ordaz becomes president.

1968   Student uprising; Tlatelolco "massacre." Mexico City hosts Olympic Games.

1970–1976   Luis Echeverría's *sexenio;* Mexico becomes third world leader.

1974   Mexico joins Venezuela in creating a Latin American economic system.

1976   Vast oil deposits found in southern Mexico and Bay of Campeche.

1976–1982   José López Portillo's *sexenio;* he uses petroleum wealth to obtain loans for rapid economic development.

1982   Miguel de la Madrid becomes president.

1982–1988   U.S. aid averts Mexico's financial collapse; Mexico opposes U.S. policy in Central America; living standards in Mexico sharply decline. Debate in United States continues over "illegal" immigration and employment of undocumented workers.

1986   U.S. Sen. Jesse Helms begins controversial Senate hearings on corruption in Mexico. Congress passes Immigration Reform and Control Law.

1988   Political crisis in Mexico. Carlos Salinas de Gortari becomes
                        president amid widespread charges of fraud.

1988–1990   Mexico joins General Agreement on Tariff and Trade;
                        United States agrees to reduce Mexico's debt interest
                        payments. Number of U.S. citizens of Mexican heritage is 15
                        million.

NOTES

Preface

1. Joint Economic Committee (100th Cong., 2d Sess.), *Economic Reform in Mexico: Implications for the United States* (Washington: Government Printing Office, 1988), 1–2.

2. Polyconomics, "Executive Summary and Recommendations," 16-page extract from *Mexico at 2000* (New Brunswick, N.J.: Polyconomics, 1990). See also the commentary by Robert Pastor in the *Los Angeles Times* (June 8, 1990); and "Salinas Takes A Gamble," *The New Republic* (September 10 & 17, 1990), 27–32.

Sydney Weintraub, *A Marriage of Convenience: Relations Between Mexico and the United States* (New York: Oxford University Press, 1990), 209, exploring the often contradictory and discouraging assessments about modern U.S.–Mexican relations, notes: "Great tension marks the United States-Mexico relationship—differences separate the two countries while their mutual dependence brings them together. The two pulls are always present."

For a sharply divergent view of Mexico's economy from a leftist perspective, see David Barkin, *Distorted Development: Mexico in the World Economy* (Boulder: Westview Press, 1990).

chapter 1

1. David Pletcher, *The Diplomacy of Annexation: Texas, Oregon, and the Mexican War* (Columbia: University of Missouri Press, 1973), is the most authoritative account in English. I have also used Carlos Bosch García, *Historia de las relaciones entre México y los Estados Unidos, 1819–1848* (Mexico City: UNAM, 1961), and Gene Brack, *Mex-*

ico Views Manifest Destiny, 1821–1846 (Albuquerque: University of New Mexico Press, 1975).

2. For Polk's strategy see Frederick Merk, *Manifest Destiny and Mission in American History: A Reinterpretation* (New York: Knopf, 1963), and *The Monroe Doctrine and American Expansionism, 1843–1849* (New York: Knopf, 1966).

3. Buchanan to Slidell, 10 November 1845, in William Ray Manning, ed., *Diplomatic Correspondence of the United States: Inter-American Affairs,* vol. 8 (Washington, D.C.: Carnegie Endowment for International Peace, 1937), 173.

4. Thomas Hietala, *Manifest Design: Anxious Aggrandizement in late Jacksonian America* (Ithaca, N.Y.: Cornell University Press, 1985), 255–57; Reginald Horsman, *Race and Manifest Destiny: The Origins of American Racial Anglo-Saxonism* (Cambridge, Mass.: Harvard Univ. Press, 1981), passim; and *New York Herald,* 11 April 1848, quoted in Robert Johannsen, *To the Halls of the Montezumas: The Mexican War in the American Imagination* (New York: Oxford University Press, 1985), 303.

5. Quoted in German Arciniegas, *Latin America: A Cultural History* (New York: Knopf, 1966), 379.

6. Agustin Cué Canovas, *Juárez, los Estados Unidos, y Europa* (Mexico City: Ediciones Centenario, 1959), 159–60. See also Alfred and Kathryn Hanna, *Napoleon III and Mexico: American Triumph over Monarchy* (Chapel Hill: University of North Carolina Press, 1971), and Thomas Schoonover, *Dollars over Dominion: The Triumph of Liberalism in Mexican–United States Relations, 1861–67* (Baton Rouge, La.: LSU press, 1978), who stresses the common economic philosophies of Republicans and Mexican Liberals.

7. David Pletcher, *Rails, Mines, and Progress: Seven American Promoters in Mexico, 1877–1911* (Ithaca, N.Y.: Cornell University Press, 1958), passim; Luis Nicolau d'Olwer, "Las inversiones extranjeras," in Daniel Cosio Villegas, ed., *Historia moderna de México,* vol. 2, *La Vida Económica* (Mexico City: Editorial Hermes, 1965).

8. Quoted in Josefina Zoraida Vázquez and Lorenzo Meyer, *The United States and Mexico* (Chicago: University of Chicago Press, 1985), 106. In the origins of the Mexico revolution I have drawn heavily on this work and Victor Alba, *The Mexicans: The Making of a Nation* (New York: Praeger, 1967), 94–139. Alan Knight provides an exhaustive summary in *The Mexican Revolution,* 2 vols. (Cambridge, Eng.: Cambridge University Press, 1986), arguing that the older interpretations of the revolution as an agrarian revolt are largely correct.

9. For much of this section I have relied on my *The Banana Wars: United States Intervention in the Caribbean, 1898–1934* (Lexington: University of Kentucky Press, 1983), esp. 77–114, but the reader may profitably follow the Veracruz affair in Robert Quirk, *An Affair of Honor: Woodrow Wilson and the Occupation of Veracruz* (Lexington: University of Kentucky, 1961); Kenneth Grieb, *The United States and Huerta* (Lincoln: University of Nebraaska Press, 1969); and Berta Ulloa, *La revolución intervenida: relaciones diplomáticas entre México y los Estados Unidos, 1910–1914* (Mexico City: El Colegio de México, 1971).

10. Huerta went to London and then sailed for New York, where he took up residence on Long Island. In 1915, with the Mexican situation still muddled, he moved

to a village north of El Paso and began plotting a return to Mexico. U.S. officials arrested him for violation of the neutrality statutes. He was tossed in jail where, severely depressed, he resumed his copious drinking. He died there in January 1916 of cirrhosis of the liver.

11. For the secret war in Mexico, see the monumental study by Friedrich Katz, *The Secret War in Mexico: Europe, the United States, and the Mexican Revolution* (Chicago: University of Chicago Press, 1981).

12. Karl M. Schmitt, *Mexico and the United States, 1821–1973* (New York: Wiley, 1973), 154–64.

13. Albert Michaels, "The Crisis of Cardenismo," *Journal of Latin American Studies* 2 (January 1970); 51–79, and Lorenzo Meyer, "Las relaciones con el exterior," in Daniel Cosio Villegas, coordinator, *Historia general de México*, vol. 2 (Mexico City: El Colegio de México, 1976), 1250–51.

chapter 2

1. Lorenzo Meyer (Muriel Vasconcillos, trans.), *Mexico and the United States in the Oil Controversy, 1917–1942* (Austin: University of Texas Press, 1977), surveys the crisis from the Mexican position. U.S. investment in Mexico declined from $1 billion in 1925 to $300 million in 1940.

2. "Guerra Mundial," Archivo de Relaciones Exteriores (hereafter ARE), 3-909-3.

3. Ibid., 3-908-2; Howard Cline, *The United States and Mexico* (Cambridge, Mass.: Harvard University Press, 1953), 247–249, 261–68; Avila Camacho, "Memorandum sobre problemas internacionales pendientes entre México y los Estados Unidos," Avila Camacho, 577/3, *Ramo Presidencial*, Archivo General de la Nación (hereafter AGN).

4. Cline, *United States and Mexico*, 268–69; "Guerra Mundial," ARE, 3-907-1.

5. Cline, *United States and Mexico*, 271–78; Raymond Vernon, *The Dilemma of Mexico's Development: The Roles of the Private and Public Sectors* (Cambridge, Mass.: Harvard University Press, 1963), 94–95; Luis G. Zorilla, *Historia de relaciones entre México y los Estados Unidos de América, 1800–1958*, vol. 2 (Mexico City: Editorial Porrúa, 1966), 502–3.

6. Ezekiel Padilla, *Expedientes Personales*, ARE, 23-27-24; Guy Ray, secretary to U.S. ambassador to Mexico, 16 March 1945, State Department, Central Files, Mexico, National Archives (hereafter NA).

7. American consul, Guadalajara, 11 January 1945, Central Files, Mexico, NA; Bohan memo, 27 January 1945, in *Foreign Relations of the United States, 1945* (hereafter *FR* and year), 9:64.

8. Messersmith to Nelson Rockefeller, 7 February 1945, *FR 1945*, 9:89. Messersmith got along well with Avila Camacho, too, but when the Mexican president requested $150 million in loans for a three- to five-year period, the ambassador politely conveyed the recommendation that the amount be significantly lowered and targeted for specific projects (ibid., 1160–69).

9. Carrigan memo, 2 July 1945 and Messersmith to Carrigan, 7 September 1945, Central Files, Mexico, NA.

10. Luis Medina, *Historia de la revolución mexicana, 1940–1952: civilismo y modernización del autoritarismo* (Mexico City: El Colego de México, 1979), 81–82; Brandenburg, *Making of Modern Mexico*, 100–1. Throughout the campaign the rumors of clandestine U.S. involvement persisted: the newspaper *El Popular* reported (18 September 1945) that three U.S. Catholic leaders (among them the archbishop of Chicago) had arrived in Mexico to persuade the National Sinarquista Union to field a candidate, and Lombardo Toledano charged that "imperialist" U.S. business firms were smuggling arms to the Sinarquistas.

11. Messersmith to acting secretary of state, 12 January 1946, *FR 1946*, 11:973.

12. Messersmith to Assistant Secretary of State Will Clayton, 27 April 1946, ibid., 1051–52.

13. Quoted in Lester D. Langley, *America and the Americas: The United States in the Western Hemisphere* (Athens: University of Georgia Press, 1989), 167.

14. James Cockcroft, *Mexico: Class Formation, Capital Accumulation, and the State* (New York: Monthly Review Press, 1983), 152–53.

15. Cockcroft argues that U.S. bankers, as creditors of the Nacional Financiera and buyers of its bonds, had "considerable influence over state economic decision making," (ibid., 184–85). For a more even-handed assessment, see Vernon, *Dilemma of Mexico's Development*, 102–3, and especially Lorenzo Meyer, "La encrucijada," in *Historia general de México* vol. 2 (Mexico City: Colegio de México, 1981), 1276–81.

16. *FR 1946*, 11:1008–1116.

17. *New York Times*, 4 March 1947.

18. Medina, *Historia de la revolución mexicana, 1940–1952*. 176–77; *New York Times*, 12, 30 April 1947.

19. Alemán headed into the American heartland to Kansas City, where a Mexican community of stockyard and railroad laborers had formed early in the century. At what is now Alemán Court in Country Club Plaza, a business district of fashionable shops and upscale restaurants, his visit is commemorated by a small plaque of Mexican tile embossed with the eagle and serpent.

20. Pedro González Casanova, *La democracia en México* (Mexico City: Ediciones Era, 1965).

21. Cline, *The United States and Mexico*, 337–42.

22. Hanson, *Politics of Mexican Development*, 72–73.

23. Cline, *The United States and Mexico*, 348–55.

chapter 3

1. Memo, 29 March 1950, *FR 1950*, 2:598–624.

2. "Why I Am Anti-Soviet and Anti-Russian," *El Nacional*, 27 April 1951.

3. Memo, 20 July 1950 and 11 August 1950, and U.S. ambassador to Mexico to secretary of state, 16 March 1951, Central Files, Mexico, NA; *New York Daily News*, 2 January 1951.

4. Memo, 6 April 1951, *FR 1951*, 2:1476–77.

5. Memo, director of the Office of Middle American Affairs, ibid., 1483. See also Zorilla, *Historia de las relaciones entre México y los Estados Unidos*, 2: 544–45.

6. 1 October 1951, *FR 1951*, 2:1489–90. As the United States began signing a series of military defense agreements with other Latin American nations under the Inter-American Treaty of Reciprocal Assistance, it pressed the Mexicans to accept a similar agreement. But Alemán, citing constitutional limitations on the dispatching of troops to foreign soil, resisted, arguing that Mexico could accept military aid under the Mexico–U.S. defense pact as a means of strengthening its national defense. After several sessions, the talks broke down.

7. Ojeda, *Política exterior de México*, 50–51, 57; Miguel Alemán 831/2503, 433/121A, *Ramo Presidencial*, AGN.

8. For example, when Mann proposed to Tello the creation of "technical groups" by the OAS for the purpose of identifying individuals and groups "dedicated to the advancement of the Soviet communist movement" in the hemisphere, Tello responded that Hitler had used something similar to deal with his enemies, then wryly noted, "If a Mexican commits a crime against his country, Mexico will punish him." Tello continued his protestations in Washington with Asst. Secretary of State Edward Miller and found him "resistant," but Secretary of State Dean Acheson, then being vilified by Sen. Joseph McCarthy, wrote Tello, evinced a "great comprehension" of Mexico's position and did not press the matter (Manuel Tello, *México: una posición internacional* [Mexico City: Mortíz, 1972], 18–20).

Even the Soviets presumed that Mexico's economic subordinance to the United States meant, inevitably, political submissiveness. In 1952, when the Mexican delegate in the United Nations proposed a solution to the impasse at the peace talks in Panmunjom, Korea, the Soviet ambassador to the United States invited Luis Quintanilla, then serving as Mexican ambassador to the United States, to his summer place near Annapolis to find out, as Quintanilla later explained, if the Americans had inspired the move. But the decision was Alemán's. The Mexican president had initially been little concerned with the haggling in Korea but subsequently decided that Mexico's best interest lay in a U.S.–Soviet agreement about Korea (Dean Acheson, memo, 24 September 1952, Central Files, Mexico, NA).

Mexico's role in the resolution of the impasse about prisoner exchange at the Panmunjom talks was important. As the movement to promote Alemán for a Nobel Peace Prize intensified, Mexico's ambassador to the United Nations, Luis Padilla Nervo, saying that Alemán was "preoccupied with the indefinite prolonging of the Korean conflict," proposed that prisoners be exchanged according to the 1949 Geneva Convention, which established the principle of nonforced repatriation (text in Secretario de relaciones exteriores, *Corea*, 12/411.1 (7) (07)/1, ARE.

9. Vázquez and Meyer, *United States and Mexico*, 168–70; Francis White to Henry Holland, 14 May and 1 June 1954, Holland Files, Lot 57D295, RG 59, NA; Ruiz Cortines, *Informe*, 162.1/3, AGN.

10. Jesús Reyes Heroles, in Ruiz Cortines 162.1/3, AGN.

11. Steven Sanderson, *The Receding Frontier: Aspects of the Internationalization of U.S.–Mexican Agriculture and Their Implications for Bilateral Relations in the 1980s* (La Jolla, Calif.: Center for U.S.–Mexican Studies, 1981), 4–11. David Montejano, *Anglos and Mexicans in the Making of Texas, 1836–1986* (Austin: University of Texas

Press, 1987), describes in stark detail the "marginalization" of the rural Mexican American in Texas. Ernesto Galarza, *Farm Workers and Agribusiness in California, 1947–1960* (Notre Dame, Ind.: University of Notre Dame Press, 1977), 8–15.

12. Juan R. García, *Operation Wetback: The Mass Deportation of Mexican Undocumented Workers in 1954* (Westport, Conn.: Greenwood, 1980), 30–31.

13. U.S. consul, Ciudad Juárez, 29 May 1947, Central Files, Mexico, NA; telephone conversation between Sánchez Gavito and Ambassador de la Colima, 6 December 1948, ARE 2486-9.

14. *New York Times*, 27 March 1951; Truman to Alemán, 14 July 1951, and letter to Alemán, n.d., Alemán, 671/14501, AGN; Mexican Workers' Conference to Ruiz Cortines, 19 January 1954, Ruiz Cortines, 548 1/122, AGN.

15. Rubottom, memo, 17 July 1950, *FR 1950*, 2: 956–57.

16. *New York Times*, 12 May 1953; Pellecer, *Historia de la revolución mexicana*, 23:117–18.

17. The exchange is in *FR 1952–1954*, 4:1339–46.

18. Pellecer, *Historia de la revolución mexicana*, 23:75; Matt Meier and Feliciano Rivera, *The Chicanos* (New York: Hill & Wang, 1972), 229.

19. Holland to the secretary of state, 31 August 1955, Holland Files, Lot 57295D, NA.

20. Banco de México, listed in Pellecer, *Historia de la revolución mexicana*, 23:32; Zorilla, *Historia de las relaciones entre México y los Estados Unidos de América*, 2:550–51.

21. Meyer, "La encruciada," in *Historia general de México*, 2:1344–45, 1350–51.

22. Vázquez and Meyer, *The United States and Mexico*, 170–72.

23. *New York Times*, 14 February 1954.

24. Office confidential memo, 25 March 1955, White, Confidential Files, 10 June 1955, and Holland memo, 12 June 1955, State Department, Central Files, NA.

25. White to Holland, 27 September 1955, Holland Files, Lot 57/295D, RG 59, NA; *New York Times*, 20 December 1955.

26. On the dilemmas confronting López Mateos, see Olga Pellicer de Brody y José Luis Reyna, *Historia de la revolución mexicana, 1952–1960: el afianzamiento de la estabilidad política* (Mexico City: El Colegio de México, 1972), 215–18.

chapter 4

1. Arthur K. Smith, "Mexico and the Cuban Revolution: Foreign Policy Making in Mexico under President Adolfo López Mateos, 1958–1964" (Ph.D. diss., Cornell University, 1970), 127–28. López's remarks appeared in the *New York Times*, 2 December 1958. Meyer, "La encrucijada," in *Historia general de México*, 2:1290–91; Frank Brandenberg, *The Making of Modern Mexico* (Englewood Cliffs, N.J.: Prentice-Hall, 1964), 116–17.

2. Olga Pellicer de Brody y Esteban L. Mancilla, *Historia de la revolución mexicana, 1952–1960: el entendimiento con los Estados Unidos y la gestación del desarrollo estabilizador* (Mexico City: El Colegio de México, 1978), 112; Mario Ojeda, *Alcances y*

límites de la política exterior de México (Mexico City: El Colegio de México, 1976), 80–81. The Mexican government, in fact, had reason to worry about Castro's premature dispatch of rebel units into the Caribbean in summer 1959. Some of these guerrillas began operating in isolated Quintana Roo in eastern Yucatán. In a major address at the United Nations in October 1959, López made clear that he identified with the cause of "peaceful revolution." Latin America, he declared, needed democracy and economic development in order to prevent the Communists from exploiting its misery and social backwardness. These were essentially the same arguments John F. Kennedy used in justifying the Alliance for Progress (*New York Times,* 12 July 1959, 15 October 1959).

3. Smith, "Mexico and the Cuban Revolution," 132–34.

4. Ibid., 168.

5. Quoted in Olga Pellecer de Brody, "Mexico in the 1970s and Its Relations with the United States," in Julio Cotler and Richard Fagen, eds., *Latin America and the United States* (Stanford, Calif.: Stanford University Press, 1974), 317. Eisenhower had commented that if the Communists came to power in Mexico because of the economic pressure on Cuba, "in all likelihood we would have to go to war about this" (Quoted in Stephen Rabe, *Eisenhower and Latin America: The Foreign Policy of Anticommunism* [Chapel Hill: University of North Carolina Press, 1988], p. 165).

6. Quoted in the *New York Times,* 8 February 1961. Despite the severity of his criticism, the *Times* editorialist meekly concluded that what Mexico needed was understanding, sympathy, and helpfulness. These were admirable but naive American traits Mexican officials sometimes exploited when dealing with Americans.

7. Smith, "Mexico and the Cuban Revolution," 170–72.

8. See, for example, Vázquez and Meyer, *United States and Mexico,* 174.

9. The Chamizal had been a festering matter for almost a century, and with the rapid growth of the El Paso/Ciudad Juárez area had acquired a political urgency. For years, farmers in the Mexicali valley of Sonora had been complaining that the American Weldon-Mohawk irrigation canals had resulted in excessive saline content of Colorado River waters flowing into Mexico and ruined crops.

10. State Department *Bulletin,* 23 July 1962, 135–37.

11. State Department, *American Foreign Policy, 1961* (Washington, D.C.: Government Printing Office, 1965), 441; *American Foreign Policy, 1962* (1966), 530. Mexico went further down on the list of foreign assistance recipients in 1963 but received almost $50 million, 50 percent of it from the Export-Import Bank.

12. Air attaché, Mexico, 26 July 1962. DeClassified Documents Catalog (81) 294A.

13. Vázquez and Meyer, *United States and Mexico,* 178–79. Mexico City was already established as "second home" for spies—Soviet, American, and now Cuban—who found Mexico an attractive base from which to carry out operations in third countries. The Mexicans, wrote David Atlee Phillips, a CIA operative stationed in Mexico City in the early 1960s, looked on these activities with "bemused tolerance," unless, of course, the spies got involved with internal matters (*The Night Watch* [New York: Atheneum, 1977], 114).

14. Vázquez and Meyer, *United States and Mexico,* 175.

15. On the conditions in rural northwestern Mexico in the late 1950s and early 1960s, see Peter Baird and Ed McCaughan, *Beyond the Border: Mexico and the U.S. Today* (New York: North American Congress on Latin America, 1979), 31–32. Richard Craig, *The Bracero Program: Interest Groups and Foreign Policy* (Austin: University of Texas Press, 1971), discusses both the internal and international dimensions of the program.

16. Craig, *Bracero Program*, 17–18; Harry Cross and James A. Sandos, *Across the Border: Rural Development in Mexico and Recent Migration to the United States* (Berkeley: University of California Press, 1981), 43.

17. Craig, *The Bracero Program*, 22–23.

18. Quoted in ibid., 173.

19. Quoted in ibid., 186.

20. "Talking Points," Johnson and López meeting, 20–22 February 1964, LBJ Library, in *DeClassified Documents;* Baird and McCaughan, *Beyond the Border,* 129–30.

21. Quoted in Donald W. Baerresen, *The Border Industrialization Program of Mexico* (Lexington, Mass.: D. C. Heath, 1971), xii.

22. Víctor Urquidi and Sofía Méndez Villarreal, "Economic Importance of Mexico's Northern Border Region," in Stanley Ross, ed., *Views across the Border: The United States and Mexico* (Albuquerque: University of New Mexico Press, 1978), 147–55. The population of the Mexican border municipalities was 2.33 million in 1970.

23. Ojeda, *La política exterior de México,* 136–37. From 1957 to 1967 the value of Mexican manufacturing increased by 120 percent and that of intermediate goods (chemicals, nonmetallic minerals) by 171 percent, but the value of goods of final consumption declined from 62 percent to 53 percent. The announced intention of maintaining import substitution was to create a modern industrial sector for an internal market, but the effect, wrote Miguel Wionczek, was to modernize Mexican agriculture at the expense of the traditional rural sector. The weak scientific/technological infrastructure—in 1960 Mexico had only six research and development experts per 100,000 population as compared with 250 in the United States—meant that Mexico had to purchase this expertise and technology at a cost of $200 million annually ("Las problemas de la trasferencia de tecnología en un marco de industrialización acelerado, el caso de México," in Max Nolff, compiler, *El desarrollo industrial latinoamerica* [Mexico City: Fondo de Cultura Económica 1974], 304–29.)

chapter 5

1. Jonathan Kandell, *La Capital: The Biography of Mexico City* (New York: Random House, 1988), 516–17.

2. Kenneth Johnson, *Mexican Democracy: A Critical View,* 3d ed. (New York: Praeger, 1984), 90; Peter Smith, *Labyrinths of Power: Political Recruitment in Twentieth-Century Mexico* (Princeton, N.J.: Princeton University Press, 1979), 44–45, 78–79.

3. Manuel Moreno Sánchez, *Crisis política de México* (Mexico City: Editorial Extemporáneos, 1970), 11–17. In a special report of October 1967, "Mexico: The Problems of Progress," the CIA noted, "Mexico's general record is one of economic progress and political stability, but unrest . . . points up two basic problems. One is

the failure to fulfill a fundamental aspiration of the Revolution of 1910—improving the lot of the peasants. . . . The second problem stems from the success of Mexico's educational system, which has brought to the expanding middle class of the generally prosperous areas to a level of sophistication that will bring it into conflict with Mexico's paternalistic system of government." (*Declassified Documents Catalog* [78] 339A)

4. Quoted in Johnson, *Mexican Democracy*, 94–95.

5. Ibid., 97–99. The Tlatelolco "massacre" has, inevitably, become metaphor as another tragic expression of Emiliano Zapata's cry to the downtrodden to burn the thrones of their oppressors, who had murderously retaliated against those who had gathered to sacrifice themselves. Octavio Paz, Mexico's foremost philosopher, traced this destructive urge to the death rituals the Aztecs carried out at Tlatelolco. It had remained a mythical feature of the Mexican psyche, and Díaz had, by his death sentence for those who had gathered at Tlatelolco, confirmed that he was prepared to act in that tradition. To "rational" observers, Mexican and foreign, such interpretations were dismissed as philosophical ramblings. But Díaz showed that he understood the hold such myths have on the Mexican psyche by appearing on national television to denounce Paz for expressing such views.

6. *New York Times*, 2 October 1988, 12.

7. Memo for President Johnson, 14 July 1967, and Notes, LBJ-Díaz Ordaz meeting, 26 October 1967, LBJ Library.

8. Yoram Shapira, *Mexican Foreign Policy under Echeverría* (Beverly Hills, Calif.: SAGE, 1978), 22–23; Robert Pastor and Jorge Castañeda, *Limits to Friendship: The United States and Mexico* (New York: Knopf, 1988), 128.

9. Honeywell, "Mexican Foreign Relations and Theory of International Politics," 44–49.

10. Ojeda, *La política exterior de México*, 68–69.

11. Cockcroft, *Mexico*, 158–59; Baird, *Beyond the Border*, 77. In 1975 the subcommittee on multinational corporations of the Senate Foreign Relations Committee reported, "The sources of multinational business power are woven tightly into the fabric of Mexican industrial organization. As consumption patterns change, [multinational corporations] are found in the fastest-growing industries while local firms are left behind. With a rate of growth faster than that of nationally-owned industry, American and other foreign subsidiaries have established or gradually taken over entire product markets—products that are in some cases very important to the effective functioning of the economy. Once entrenched, subsidiaries generally operate under the close supervision and coordination of the parent" (*Multinational Corporations in Brazil and Mexico: Structural Sources of Economic and Noneconomic Power*, [Washington: Government Printing Office, 1975], 94).

12. Honeywell, "Mexican Foreign Relations and Theory of International Politics," 50–52.

13. Cockcroft, *Mexico*, 250.

14. Honeywell, "Mexican Foreign Relations and the Theory of International Politics," 53–54.

15. Juan Miguel de Mora, *Esto nos dió López Portillo* (Mexico City: Anuya Editores 1982), 31.

16. Quoted in ibid., 32.

17. Quoted in Pastor and Castañeda, *Limits to Friendship: The United States and Mexico*, 100.

18. Quoted in Mora, *Esto nos dió López Portillo*, 34, 37–8.

19. Pastor and Castañeda, *Limits to Friendship*, 100–2.

chapter 6

1. Pastor and Castañeda, *Limits of Friendship*, 103.

2. Ibid., 104–5.

3. On these points see J. Teichman, *From Boom to Bust: Policy Making in Mexico* (Boston: Unwin Hyman, 1988). One of the first things de la Madrid did after becoming president was to go after Díaz, who was subsequently convicted of embezzlement.

4. Pastor and Castañeda, *Limits of Friendship*, 106–7.

5. Ibid., 109.

6. In amendments to the immigration law of 1965, which had accorded a quota of 120,000 to the entire Western Hemisphere, the limit was set at 20,000 for each country. Though there remained special categories by which a sending nation could exceed that limit, Mexico suffered by the alteration. The effect was, in part, to exacerbate the problem of illegal entry of Mexicans or other nationals via the Mexican border.

7. Jimmy Carter, *Keeping Faith: Memoirs of a President* (New York: Bantam 1982), 468.

8. George Grayson, *Oil and Mexican Foreign Policy* (Pittsburgh: University of Pittsburgh Press, 1988), 32. Even as the Mexican economy began to deteriorate, López did not retreat from his championing of the Cubans. In 1980, shortly after the dramatic exodus of 125,000 Cubans (the "Marielitos") to Miami, an event that ended the short-lived Cuban–American dialogue, López went to Havana and pledged Mexico's solidarity with Cuba before a throng of 1 million. There followed an agreement on energy development and a $100 million loan in 1981 to help Castro pay some of his Western creditors.

9. Olga Pellecer, "Política hacia centroamérica e interés en México," in Trinidad Martínez Tarragó and Mauricio Campillo Illanes, compilers, *Centroamérica: crisis y política internacional* (Mexico City: Centro de Investigaciones y Docencia Económica, 1982), 227–52.

10. "Mexico y la crisis financiera internacional," part 2 of *Cuadernos de Política Exterior Mexicana* (1 May 1984): 43–90.

11. Sarah H. Brown, "F. Ray Marshall and the Development of Foreign Temporary Worker Policy in the Carter White House," in *Proceedings and Papers of the Georgia Association of Historians* (1989), 25–38.

12. Honeywell, "Mexican Foreign Relations," 75–76.

13. Ibid., 81–93. A parallel development was the strengthening of the place of the Mexican military within the government and a significantly broader definition of national security. As the Mexican secretary of defense said in 1980, "I understand by national security the maintenance of social, economic, and political equilibrium, guaranteed by the armed forces" (quoted in ibid., 96).

In its campaign in Guerrero, a poor state in southern Mexico where a guerrilla movement had mobilized in the early 1970s, the military had moved beyond its traditional role in maintaining order to taking civic action. It served as mediator in rural social conflict and became an indispensable part of the civilian government's efforts to expand social and economic services to rural people. In adopting civic action, the Mexican military was emulating similar programs—many of them sustained by U.S. military assistance—in other Latin American countries. By the 1980s, when rural conflict erupted in virtually every state of Mexico, the Mexican military—stripped of its political role in the early 1940s—had emerged as an institutional force in national life. See José Luis Pineyro, *Ejército y sociedad en México: pasado y presente* (Puebla, Mexico: Universidad Autónoma de Puebla, 1985).

14. Much of this section on the debate about immigration reform relies heavily on Thomas Weyr, *Hispanic U.S.A.: Breaking the Melting Pot* (New York: Harper and Row, 1988), esp. 15–50.

15. María Rosa García Acevedo, "La recuperación del control de las fronteras en Estados Unidos: implicaciones para México," in Olga Pellicer, ed., *La política exterior de México: Desafíos en los ochenta* (Mexico City: El Colegio de México, 1983), 181–84. For a more forceful expression of the Mexican position, see U.S. House and Senate Delegations, *Twenty-Second Mexico–United States Interparliamentary Conference* (Washington: Government Printing Office, 1983), 10–11. On the issue of worker migration, López Portillo declared, "We see it as a problem of commerce, a problem of finance, a problem of development, a problem of demography. . . . We cannot resolve it as a police problem" (quoted in Carlos Vázquez and Manuel García, eds., *Mexico–United States Relations: Conflict and Convergence* [Los Angeles: UCLA Chicano Studies Research Center, 1984], 67).

16. Vernon Briggs, Jr., *Mexican Migration and the U.S. Labor Market* (Austin: University of Texas Press, 1975), 26–27.

17. Kenneth Roberts, "Technology Transfer in the Mexican Bajío: Seeds, Sorghum, and Socioeconomic Change," in Ina Rosenthal-Urey, ed., *Regional Impacts of U.S.–Mexican Relations* (La Jolla, Calif.: Center for U.S.-Mexican Studies, 1986), 65–67.

18. For a penetrating study of the social consequences of Mixteca migration see Michael Kearney, "Integration of the Mixteca and the Western U.S.–Mexico Region via Migratory Wage Labor," in ibid., 71–102.

epilogue

1. U.S. Senate (99th Cong., 2d Sess.), Committee on Foreign Relations, Subcommittee on Western Hemisphere Affairs, *Situation in Mexico* (Washington: Government Printing Office, 1986), 1–3.

2. "Mexico Deserves Full U.S. Attention," *New York Times*, 17 June 1986.

3. *Situation in Mexico*, 9. One Drug Enforcement Agency casualty was Enrique Camarena, who in early 1985 was abducted in broad daylight in Guadalajara, taken to a ranch 60 miles southeast of the city, tortured, and killed. The Camarena case became a cause célèbre in Washington when Mexican officials obstructed the investigation. Although there was undeniable official complicity in the matter, the Camarena case served again to distract the American public's attention from a) the number of Mexican casualties in this "war"; b) the indirect complicity of U.S. agencies (the State Department and CIA) in drug trafficking—a consequence of the department's wishes not to offend another government and the CIA's increasing dependence on narcotics traffickers as intelligence sources; and, most disturbingly, c) the power of the drug cartel.

4. James Mills, *The Underground Empire: Where Crime and Governments Embrace* (New York: Doubleday, 1986), 1156–57.

5. Quoted in Joseph F. Demetrius, Edward Tregurtha, and Scott MacDonald, "A Brave New World," *Journal of Interamerican Studies and World Affairs* 28 (Summer 1986): 20.

6. Ibid., 21–23.

7. Joint Economic Committee (100th Cong., 2d Sess.), *Economic Reform in Mexico: Implications for the United States* (Washington: Government Printing Office, 1988), 1.

8. Ibid., 2.

9. Jaime Pérez Mendoza, "Frente a la soberbia oficial crece la indignación en Chihuahua," *Proceso*, 28 July 1986, 7–12.

10. Jorge G. Castañeda, "The Choices Facing Mexico," in Susan Kaufman Purcell, *Mexico in Transition: Essays from Both Sides of the Border* (New York: Council on Foreign Relations, 1988), 18–30.

11. Ibid., 22–24.

12. Quoted in ibid., vi–vii.

13. For differing views on what these and other changes portend for U.S. policy, see Sol Sanders, *Mexico: Chaos on Our Doorstep* (Washington: University Press of America, 1986), esp. 1–12; and Cathryn L. Thorup, ed., *The United States and Mexico: Face to Face with the New Technology* (New Brunswick, N.J.: Transaction, 1987), esp. 1–37. For a dispiriting assessment of the social crisis on the border, see Sandy Tolan, "The Border Boom: Hope and Despair," *New York Times Magazine* (1 July 1990), 17–21, 31, 40.

14. Curiously, Salinas's economic policies (including the Pacto, which called for a freeze on wages and prices, reduction of the deficit, privatization, and import liberalization, prompting cries that Mexico would be turned into another Puerto Rico) aroused concerns among some U.S. economists that Mexico was on the way to becoming another Taiwan—not a debt problem, but a trade problem. Already, in the Mexican auto industry and in the border *maquiladoras*, the Asian connection has become more visible (U.S. Congress, Joint Economic Committee, *Economic Reform in Mexico*, 56–58).

15. Thorup, "Overview," in *The United States and Mexico*, 2–4. Lamentably, the environmental and health conditions of the border have severely deteriorated, some of

it attributable to dumping by the *maquiladoras*. The Rio Grande below El Paso and especially downstream from Laredo/Nuevo Laredo is dangerously polluted, yet people drink its waters. The New River carries toxic substances from Mexicali into the Salton Sea in the Imperial Valley of California. Along the Texas border, Mexican *colonias* are sprouting, their residents buying small parcels and digging shallow wells that are soon contaminated by nearby septic tanks. El Paso County has 400 *colonias*.

16. In one respect—demographic structure by age and sex—Mexico retains its pyramidal features and will continue to do so until 2020. The decline in infant mortality rates combined with heavy population growth in the 1960s and 1970s means that Mexico must create some 800,000 to 1 million new jobs annually, which in turn requires a growth rate of 4 percent to 6 percent to *stabilize* the unemployment rate. By contrast, the United States lacks sufficient numbers of entry-level workers to fill the new jobs that will be created in the 1990s.

This statistic, inevitably, has produced befuddling interpretations about immigration and U.S. dependence on Mexican workers. Scenario A: If Mexico fails to create employment for these workers, they will "flood" northward. Scenario B: The United States needs these workers to fill anticipated shortages of entry-level workers in its economy in the 1990s.

17. Quoted in Committee for Improved U.S.–Mexican Relations, "State of Insurrection in Mexico: A Major Threat to the United States." *New York Times*, 17 October 1988.

18. Wayne Cornelius, *Los Angeles Times*, 15 May 1989.

19. Adolfo Gilly, "El régimen mexicano en su dilemma," *Nexos* (February 1990): 35–37.

20. Ibid., 41–44.

BIBLIOGRAPHIC ESSAY

This book is based largely on published sources in English and Spanish, but I have carried out limited research in the following archives: In Mexico I have used the Archivo Relaciones Exteriores, whose records are reasonably well-indexed and open to qualified researchers to about 1963, and the Archivo de la Nación, which contains the Presidential Papers (also indexed). In the National Archives of the United States I have used the Department of State, Central Files, 1945–59, Mexico, Internal Affairs; the files of the Select Committee on Immigration (Hesburgh Committee), Department of Justice; and the files of the Employment Security Agency and War Manpower Commission, Department of Labor.

Among published government documents, the following proved most useful: Instituto Nacional de Estadísticas Geográfica e Informática, *Estadísticas históricos de México* (Mexico City: Instituto Nacional de Antropología e Historia 1985); the presidential *Informes;* and the five-volume series commemorating the 175-year anniversary of Mexican independence and the 75-year anniversay of the Mexican revolution, *Política exterior de México* Mexico City: Secretaría de Relaciones Exteriores, 1985). Department of State, *Foreign Relations of the United States* (Washington, D.C.: Government Printing Office, 1861–   ), is fundamental but, given the nature of the U.S.– Mexican relationship, should be supplemented with other government documents, especially U.S. Congress hearings and reports on immigration. For the U.S. House of Representatives see *Demographic Impact of Immigration on the United States: Hearings,* two parts (Washington, D.C.: Government Printing Office, 1985); *Western Hemisphere Immigration: Hearings* (Washington, D.C.: Government Printing Office, 1975– 76); *Illegal Aliens: Hearings* (Washington, D.C.: Government Printing Office, 1972); *Immigration Reform and Control Act of 1983* (Washington, D.C.: Government Printing Office, 1983); *Hispanic Immigration and Select Committee on Immigration's Final Report* (Washington, D.C.: Government Printing Office, 1981); *Legal and Illegal Immigration to the United States* (Washington, D.C.: Government Printing Office, 1978); and *Immigration Statistics: Hearing* (Washington, D.C.: Government Printing Office,

1985). For the U.S. Senate the reader should consult *Developments in Mexico and U.S.–Mexican Relations: Hearings* and *Situation in Mexico: Hearings* (Washington, D.C.: Government Printing Office, 1986); *U.S. Immigration Policy and the National Interest* (Washington, D.C.: Government Printing Office, 1981); and *U.S. Economic Growth and Third World Debt* (Washington, D.C.: Government Printing Office, 1986). The annual publication of the Mexico–U.S. Parliamentary Conferences dates from 1961. This series should be supplemented with Donald Wyman, *The U.S. Congress and the Making of U.S. Policy toward Mexico* (La Jolla, Calif.: Center for U.S.–Mexican Studies, 1981), and José Iturriaga, *México en el Congreso de los Estados Unidos* (Mexico City: Fondo de Cultura Económica, 1988).

Among the several general histories of U.S.–Mexican diplomatic relations, the most factual is Karl Schmitt, *Mexico and the United States, 1821–1973* (New York: John Wiley, 1974), which can be supplemented with Robert Jones Shafer and Donald Mabry, *Neighbors: Mexico and the United States* (Chicago: Nelson-Hall, 1981); George Grayson, *The United States and Mexico: Patterns of Influence* (New York: Praeger, 1981); and Richard Erb and Stanley Ross, eds., *U.S. Relations with Mexico: Context and Content* (Washington, D.C.: American Enterprise Institute, 1981). For the Mexican perspective, a brief but very suggestive work is Josefina Vázquez and Lorenzo Meyer, *The United States and Mexico* (Chicago: University of Chicago Press, 1985). The Mexican counterpart to Schmitt's work is Luis Zorilla, *Historia de las relaciones entre México y los Estados Unidos, 1800–1958*, 2 vols. (Mexico City: Editorial Porrua, 1965–66). Howard F. Cline, *The United States and Mexico* (Cambridge, Mass.: Harvard Univeresity Press, 1963), remains a classic though it is rapidly becoming dated. In a special category is Robert Pastor and Jorge Castañeda, *Limits to Friendship: The United States and Mexico* (New York: Knopf, 1988), which is less a history than an enlightened dialogue between two prominent political scientists.

There is an arguable presumption that the United States has no foreign policy toward Mexico and a parallel view that Mexico has no foreign policy concerns beyond the United States, which is unarguably false. Since World War II the evolution of Mexican internationalism has been impressive, to which the number and quality of Mexican periodicals devoted to foreign relations attest. Among the best of these are *Foro Internacional, Cuadernos de Política Exterior Mexicana,* and the special issues on *México–Estados Unidos* published at the prestigious El Colegio de México. The most persuasive introduction to Mexican foreign policy is Mario Ojeda, *Alcances y límites de la política exterior de México* (Mexico City: El Colegio de México, 1976), which has largely superseded two other studies: Jorge Castañeda, *México y el orden internacional* (Mexico City: El Colegio de México, 1956), and Manuel Tello, *México: una posición internacional* (Mexico City: Mortíz, 1972). For Mexico's policy toward Cuba, see Enrique Corominas, *México, Cuba, y la O.E.A.* (Buenos Aires: Ediciones Política, Económica, Finanzas, 1965), and especially Olga Pellicer de Brody, *México y la revolución cubana* (Mexico City: El Colegio de México, 1972). George Grayson, one of the prominent Mexicanists in the United States, assesses the impact of the petroleum boom in *Oil and Mexican Foreign Policy* (Pittsburgh: University of Pittsburgh Press, 1988). Yoram Shapira interprets the internationalism of the early 1970s in *Mexican Foreign Policy under Echeverría* (Beverly Hills, Calif.: Sage, 1978), and Arthur K. Smith unravels many of the complexities of the López Mateos years in "Mexico and the Cuban Revolution: Foreign Policy Making in Mexico under President Adolfo

López Mateos (Ph.D. diss., Cornell University, Ithaca, N.Y., 1970). Blanca Torres explores Mexico's important role in World War II in *México en la segunda guerra mundial* (Mexico City: El Colegio de México, 1979).

In recent years the literature on U.S.–Mexican relations, especially in the economic context, has grown enormously. It may be properly divided into several subgroupings.

The first is interpretive didactic literature, which is occasionally suggestive but too often hortatory or despairing that any change in U.S.–Mexican affairs is possible or even desirable.

Those looking for insights into the "Mexican character" should begin with such writers as Octavio Paz, Samuel Ramos, Carlos Fuentes, Carlos Monsiváis, and Leopoldo Zea, whose works have been published in English. For the evolution of the modern Mexican state, the following are essential reading: Frank Brandenburg, *The Making of Modern Mexico* (Englewood Cliffs, N.J.: Prentice-Hall, 1964), who did such a thorough analysis that, legend has it, the Mexican government paid him not to undertake a sequel; Victor Alba, *The Mexicans: The Making of a Nation* (New York: Praeger, 1967), which offers an accessible overview; and James Wilkie, *The Mexican Revolution: Federal Expenditure and Social Change since 1910* (Berkeley: University of California Press, 1970), which documents the successes and failures in social policy since the Revolution. Howard Cline, *Mexico: Revolution to Evolution, 1940–1950* (New York: Oxford, 1963), has lost some of its original authoritativeness about Mexico in the postwar years. The reader looking for the basics on Mexican politics will be rewarded by Wayne Cornelius and Ann Craig, *Politics in Mexico: An Introduction and Overview* (La Jolla, Calif.: Center for U.S.-Mexican Studies, 1984), but should follow with Kenneth Johnson, *Mexican Democracy: A Critical View* 3d ed. (New York: Praeger, 1984). Pablo González Casanova, *La democracia en México* (Mexico City: Ediciones Era, 1965), is a reformist appeal for the unfulfilled revolutionary promise.

One of the legacies of the early Reagan years was the Bilateral Commission on the Future of U.S.–Mexican Relations, *The Challenge of Interdependence: Mexico and the United States* (Washington, D.C.: Government Printing Office, 1989). Alan Knight complements his superb two-volume study of the Mexican revolution in *U.S.–Mexican Relations, 1910–1940* (La Jolla, Calif.: Center for U.S.-Mexican Studies, 1988); Isidro Fabela comments on the postwar relationship in *Buena y mala vecindad* (Mexico City: Editorial América Nueva, 1958); Olga Pellecer de Brody explains the conflictual 1970s by reinterpreting the 1945–70 era in "Mexico in the 1970s and its Relations with the United States," in *Latin America and the United States*, ed. Julio Cotler and Richard Fagen (Stanford, Calif.: Stanford University Press, 1974), 314–34; and Carlos Vazquez and Manuel García offer a sampling of material for the 1980s in *Mexico–United States Relations: Conflict and Convergence* (Los Angeles: UCLA Chicano Studies, 1984). Varied views on changes in modern Mexico and what they mean are offered in Susan Kaufman Purcell, ed., *Mexico in Transition: Implications for U.S. Policy* (New York: Council on Foreign Relations, 1988); Judith Hellman, *Mexico in Crisis* (New York: Holmes and Meier, 1983); and Peter Smith, *Mexico: Neighbor in Transition* (New York: Foreign Policy Association, 1984). Those looking for validation of their pessimism will find it in Elaine Shannon, *Desperados: Latin Drug Lords, U.S. Lawmen, and the War America Can't Win* (New York: Viking, 1988), and especially in Sol Sanders, *Mexico: Chaos on Our Doorstep* (Washington, D.C.: University Press of America, 1986). Those who wish a readable introduction to modern Mexico and its people will find it in Alan Riding, *Distant Neighbors: A Portrait of the Mexicans* (New

York: Vintage, 1986), and Patrick Oster, *The Mexicans: A Personal Portrait of a People* (New York: Morrow, 1988).

The economic literature is duller but more informative. The reader may begin with general books and collections, such as Peggy Musgrove, ed., *Mexico and the United States: Studies in Economic Intervention* (Boulder, Colo.: Westview, 1985); Barry Poulson and T. Noel Osborn, eds., *U.S.–Mexico Economic Relations* (Boulder, Colo.: Westview, 1979); Clark Reynolds and Carlos Tello, eds., *U.S.–Mexico Relations: Economic and Social Aspects* (Stanford, Calif.: Stanford University Press, 1983); Cathryn Thorup, ed., *The United States and Mexico: Face to Face with the New Technology* (New Brunswick, N.J.: Transaction, 1987); Jorge Domínguez, *Mexico's Political Economy: Challenges at Home and Abroad* (Beverly Hills, Calif.: Sage 1982); and Khosrow Fatemi, ed., *U.S.–Mexican Economic Relations: Problems and Prospects* (New York: Praeger, 1988). Some of the older studies on the Mexican political economy— particularly Raymond Vernon, *The Dilemma of Mexico's Development: The Roles of the Private and Public Sectors* (Cambridge, Mass.: Harvard University Press, 1963); Roger Hansen, *The Politics of Mexican Development* (Baltimore: Johns Hopkins University Press, 1971); and William P. Glade, Jr., and Charles W. Anderson, *The Political Economy of Mexico* (Madison: University of Wisconsin Press, 1963)—remain basic reading. Those pursuing the issue of economic development and income should begin with Pedro Aspe and Paul Sigmund, *The Political Economy of Income Distribution in Mexico* (New York: Holmes and Meier, 1984). An increasingly important issue in analyses of modern Mexico is the role of the military, a topic authoritatively explored in David Ronfeldt, *The Modern Mexican Military: Implications for Mexico's Stability and Security* (La Jolla, Calif.: Center for U.S.-Mexican Studies, 1985), a Rand Corporation study.

From this starting point, the reader may pursue various economic subthemes, many of them treated authoritatively in the publications of the Center for U.S.–Mexican Studies at La Jolla, California. Since 1982 the center (now joined by the Colegio de Frontera Norte) has published the *International Guide to Research on Mexico*.

For agriculture and the agrarian question see Steven Sanderson, *The Receding Frontier: Aspects of the Internationalization of U.S.–Mexican Agriculture and Their Implications for Bilateral Relations in the 1980s* (La Jolla, Calif.: Center for U.S.-Mexican Studies, 1981); idem., *The Transformation of Mexican Agriculture: International Structure and the Politics of Rural Change* (Princeton, N.J.: Princeton University Press, 1986); Rose Spalding, *The Mexican Food Crisis: An Analysis of the SAM* (La Jolla, Calif.: Center for U.S.-Mexican Studies, 1984); Cassio Luiselli Fernández, *The Mexican Food System: Elements of a Program of Accelerated Production of Basic Foodstuffs* (La Jolla, Calif.: Center for U.S.-American Studies, 1981); idem., *The Route to Food Self-Sufficiency in Mexico: Interactions with the U.S. Food System* (La Jolla, Calif.: Center for U.S.-Mexican Studies, 1985); and Merilee Grindle, *Bureaucrats, Politicians, and Peasants in Mexico: A Case Study in Public Policy* (Berkeley: University of California Press, 1977), which is basic. On the link between agricultural development and migration see Kenneth Roberts, *Agrarian Structure and Labor Migration in Rural Mexico* (La Jolla, Calif.: Center for U.S.-Mexican Studies, 1981), and Bruce Johnston et al., *U.S.–Mexican Relations: Agriculture and Rural Development* (Stanford, Calif.: Stanford University Press, 1987).

The official view on Mexican economic policy is detailed in *Mexico: National*

Industrial Development Plan, 2 vols. (London: Graham and Trotman, 1979). Others are Judith A. Telchman, *Policymaking in Mexico: From Boom to Crisis* (Winchester, Mass.: Unwin Hyman, 1988), which plots the downturn in the 1980s; James D. Cockcroft, *Mexico: Class Formation, Capital Accumulation, and the State* (New York: Monthly Review Press, 1983), is a Marxist analysis; Leopoldo Solís, *Economic Policy Reform in Mexico: A Case Study for Developing Countries* (New York: Pergamon, 1981); Dale Story, *Industry, the State, and Public Policy in Mexico* (Austin: University of Texas Press, 1986); Sanford Mosk, *Industrial Revolution in Mexico* (Berkeley: University of California Press, 1954), which remains useful for the critical postwar years; *Mexico's Recent Economic Growth: The Mexican View* (Austin: University of Texas Press, 1967); Nora Hamilton and Timothy Harding, eds., *Modern Mexico: State, Economy, and Social Conflict* (Beverly Hills, Calif.: Sage, 1986), which contains articles from the periodical *Latin American Perspectives;* Peter Gregory, *The Myth of Market Failure: Employment and the Labor Market in Mexico* (Baltimore: Johns Hopkins University Press, 1986), which questions the long-held view that Mexican economic policy failed to create an internal market; and Jesús Agustín Velasco, *Impact of Mexican Oil Policy on Economic and Political Development* (Lexington, Mass.: D. C. Heath, 1983).

On multinational corporations in Mexico see Lorenzo Meyer, *Las empresas trans-nacionales de México* (Mexico City: El Colegio de México, 1974); Bernardo Sepúlveda et al., *Las empresas transnacionales en México* (Mexico City: El Colegio de México, 1974); Bernardo Sepúlveda and Antonio Chumacero, *La inversión extranjera en México* (Mexico City: Fondo de Cultura Económica, 1973); and Harry K. Wright, *Foreign Enterprise in Mexico* (Chapel Hill: University of North Carolina Press, 1971).

Regarding trade issues, Bernhard Fischer, Egbert Gerken, and Ulrich Hiemenz, *Growth, Employment, and Trade in an Industrializing Economy* (Tübingen, West Germany: Institut für Weltwirtschaften der Universität Kiel, 1982), is technical; more accessible are *U.S. Finance and Trade Links with Less-Developed Countries* (Austin: Lyndon B. Johnson School of Public Affairs, 1984), and especially John F. H. Purcell, *Trade Conflicts and U.S.–Mexican Relations* (La Jolla, Calif.: Center for U.S.-Mexican Studies, 1982). Sidney Weintraub responds affirmatively in *Free Trade between Mexico and the United States?* (Washington, D.C.: Brookings Institute, 1984)

The U.S.–Mexican border, it is often said, has been "studied to death," a comment seemingly validated by the enormity of the literature. Serious students should begin with the first-rate bibliographic guide, Barbara G. Valk et al., *Borderline: A Bibliography of the United States–Mexico Borderlands* (Los Angeles: University of California Press, 1988), which lists "books, serial titles, journal articles, chapters and sections of books, government documents, conference proceedings, theses and dissertations, unpublished papers, maps, films, and other audiovisual materials" (most of them published from 1960 to 1985) in the sciences, social sciences, and humanities focusing on the four U.S. and six Mexican states comprising the U.S.–Mexican border and such broader topics as U.S.–Mexican relations and immigration.

General works on the border are Oscar Martínez, *Troublesome Border* (Tucson, Ariz.: University of Arizona Press, 1988), which argues that the border has been historically a conflictual zone; John W. House, *Frontier on the Rio Grande: A Political Geography of Development and Social Deprivation* (Oxford, Eng.: Clarendon Press, 1982), which is authoritative; and Alan Weisman, *La frontera: The United States Border with Mexico* (San Diego: Harcourt Brace Jovanovich, 1984), which offers a moving account of life on the border. Stanley Ross, ed., *Views across the Border: The United States and Mexico* (Albuquerque: University of New Mexico Press, 1978), strives for a scholarly rebuttal to the damning indictment in Ovid Demaris, *Poso del mundo* (Boston: Little, Brown, 1970).

Sharply conflicting views about the *maquiladora* program appear in Donald Baerrensen, *The Border Industrialization Program of Mexico* (Lexington, Mass.: D. C. Heath, 1971), which is supportive, and Peter Baird and Ed McCaughen, *Beyond the Border: Mexico and the United States Today* (New York: North American Congress on Latin America, 1979), a publication of the North American Conference on Latin America. A recent study on the *maquiladora* program is Leslie Sklair, *Assembling for Development: The Maquila Industry in Mexico and the United States* (Boston: Unwin Hyman, 1989), which should be supplemented with Niles Hansen, *The Border Economy: Regional Development in the Southwest* (Austin: University of Texas Press, 1981); and Lay J. Gibson and Alfonso Corona Rentería, *The United States and Mexico: Borderland Development and the National Economies* (Boulder, Colo.: Westview, 1985). Two urban studies are Oscar Martínez, *Border Boom Town: Ciudad Juárez since 1880* (Los Angeles: University of California Press, 1975), and John Price, *Tijuana: Urbanization in a Border Culture* (Notre Dame, Ind.: University of Notre Dame Press, 1973).

Migration is an old not a new issue in U.S.–Mexican relations, and the reader should begin with the classics, among them Manuel Gamio, *The Mexican Immigrant* (New York: Arno, 1969; orig. pub., 1931); Carey McWilliams, *Ill Fares the Land* (Boston: Houghton Mifflin, 1942); idem., *North from Mexico: The Spanish-Speaking People of the United States* (New York: Lippincott, 1949), updated edition by Matt Meier published by Greenwood Press, Westwood, Conn., in 1989; and Paul Taylor, *An American–Mexican Frontier: Nueces County, Texas* (1934; New York: Russell and Russell, 1971). The modern debate over immigration can be followed in Richard Lamm and Gary Imhoff, *The Immigration Time Bomb: The Fragmenting of America* (New York: E. P. Dutton, 1985), which set off a storm of criticism from Hispanics; David Reimers, *Still the Golden Door: The Third World Comes to America* (New York: 1985), which details the impact of the 1985 immigration law; Wayne Cornelius, director of the U.S.–Mexico Studies at The University of California, San Diego, *Immigration, Mexican Development Policy, and the Future of U.S.–Mexican Relations* (La Jolla, Calif.: Center for U.S.-Mexican Studies, 1981); Peter Brown and Henry Shue, eds., *The Border That Joins: Mexican Migrants and U.S. Responsibility* (Boston: Rowman and Littlefield, 1983), which makes the case for a benevolent policy; Centro de Estudios Internacionales, Colegio de México, *Indocumentados: mitos y realidades* (Mexico City: El Colegio de México, 1979), which disputes the commonly held notion that the undocumented were remaining in the United States; and Thomas Muller and Thomas Espenshade, *The Fourth Wave: California's Newest Immigrants* (Washington, D.C.: Urban Institute Press, 1985), which analyzes the economic impact and social costs of the immigrants and concludes that California profitted from their presence. For the rebuttal of an economist, addressing the central question of the undocumented in the labor market, see Vernon Briggs, *Mexican Migration and the U.S. Labor Market: A Mounting Issue for the Seventies* (Austin: University of Texas Press, 1975).

INDEX

THE AUTHOR

Lester D. Langley is research professor at the University of Georgia, where he has taught Latin American history since 1970. He served as Fulbright lecturer at the Universidad Rodrigo Facio in Costa Rica in 1986 and at the Instituto de Historia of the Universidad Católica de Valparaíso (Chile) in 1989. He has published 10 books on U.S.–Latin American relations, including a two-volume history of the United States and the Caribbean and an interpretation of the Isthmian crisis, *Central America: The Real Stakes* (1985). Currently he serves as general editor for the series "The United States and the Americas" and has published the general volume for that series, *America and the Americas: The United States in the Western Hemisphere* (1989).

Professor Langley is a frequent visitor to Mexico and in 1988 published his first book on Mexico, *MexAmerica: Two Countries, One Future,* to be published in a Spanish edition by the Fondo de Cultura Económica.